Great Bible Characters:
Paul

by

Bobby L. Graham

ISBN 1-58427-1787

978-158427-178-09

Guardian of Truth Foundation
P.O. Box 9670
Bowling Green, Kentucky 42101
1-800-428-0121
www.truthbooks.net

Table of Contents

Young Saul Grows Up

From the relative obscurity of his childhood to the prominence of Judaism's major persecutor to the elevation given him by Jesus Christ, the story of Paul is a fascinating one. No one interested in a study of biblical characters would dare to neglect the thrilling life of Paul, given his major role in the inspired historical record of Luke in Acts of the Apostles and his contribution of at least thirteen books to the New Testament library.

Yet when we meet him in the New Testament narrative of Acts 7:58, he is Saul, only later to become the Paul whom the world knows and acclaims. While there is much that we will never know of his early years until we share in the everlasting scenes of that eternal city, we can learn something of his childhood and youth from scattered references of the New Testament.

Passages to Consider

I am indeed a Jew, born in Tarsus of Cilicia, but brought up in this city at the feet of Gamaliel, taught according to the strictness of our fathers' law, and was zealous toward God as you all are today (Acts 22:3).

But when Paul perceived that one part were Sadducees and the other Pharisees, he cried out in the council, "Men *and* brethren, I am a Pharisee, the son of a Pharisee; concerning the hope and resurrection of the dead I am being judged!" (Acts 23:6).

My manner of life from my youth, which was spent from the beginning among my own nation at Jerusalem, all the Jews know (Acts 26:4).

Are they Hebrews? So am I. Are they Israelites? So am I. Are they the seed of Abraham? So am I (2 Cor. 11:22).

For you have heard of my former conduct in Judaism, how I persecuted the church of God beyond measure and tried *to* destroy it (Gal. 1:13).

. . . circumcised the eighth day, of the stock of Israel, of the tribe of Benjamin, a Hebrew of the Hebrews; concerning the law, a Pharisee; concerning zeal, persecuting the church; concerning the righteousness which is in the law, blameless (Phil. 3:5-6).

> **For you have heard of my former conduct in Judaism, how I persecuted the church of God beyond measure and tried to destroy it (Gal. 1:13).**

And I thank Christ Jesus our Lord who has enabled me, because He counted me faithful, putting me into the ministry, although I was formerly a blasphemer, a persecutor, and an insolent man; but I obtained mercy because I did it ignorantly in unbelief (1 Tim.1:12-13).

I thank God, whom I serve with a pure conscience, as my forefathers did, as without ceasing I remember you in my prayers night and day (2 Tim. 1:3).

His Ancestry and Family

Any mention of Saul's ancestry or family is here incorporated only for its historical significance or spiritual influence. After all, this very character being studied later voiced strong opposition to the pride of race and genealogy which was often observed in his fellow Jews. In fact, he pointedly protested the endless genealogies and Jewish fables to which many of his kinsmen resorted in their attempts to buttress the Jewish role and standing in God's plan (1 Tim. 1:3-4; Tit. 1:14; 3:9). Theirs was a distinction not grounded in God's will and way, whereas Paul's occasional reference to such matters in his writings demonstrated his refusal to depend upon these matters, though he loved his kinsmen and profited from their influence.

In passages like Romans 9:1-5; 2 Corinthians 11:22; and Philippians 3:1-7, it becomes clear that there was sufficient ground in his own family background and life for

Saul's boasting in human ancestry, race, and achievement, had he been so inclined. The last passage likely suggests that such boasting characterized Saul's earlier life, though he had sacrificed it all for the sake of gaining Christ, resulting in his glorying only in the Lord (1 Cor. 1:29-31). Only from a human perspective could one ever justify such boasting; in the face of divine law, each human being stands condemned under the guilt of his own sin and disqualified to boast (Rom. 3:27).

Saul was not merely a first-generation Pharisee, but the son of a Pharisee, though we know little else of his father (Acts 23:6). He was also able to identify his Jewish descendants all the way back to Abraham (2 Cor. 11:22). Observe the various indicators of family and ancestral background mentioned by Paul in Romans 9:4: adoption, glory, covenants, giving of the law, service of God, promises, and Christ as descendant. These advantages constitute the rich and proud heritage which Saul gave up to follow Jesus Christ, in whom there is neither Jew nor Greek, but spiritual descent from Abraham (Gal. 3:28-29).

Saul's father, who must have been responsible for the young boy's strict training as a Jew, must have been a Roman citizen, because Saul was born a citizen (Acts 22:28). While the family of Saul was part of the Diaspora (Jews dispersed among the Greeks), in Paul's claim to be "a Hebrew (born—BLG) of the Hebrews," found in Philippians 3:5, we have evidence that they had not assimilated into Greek culture but had remained faithful to their language, customs, and religious practice. As part of the tribe of Benjamin, he bore the name of the tribe's most illustrious member and king, Saul son of Kish, whether intentionally or not. His mother is most likely also included in the long, pious line of ancestors who were credited by him with influence on his own life in 2 Timothy 1:3. She undoubtedly had a large role in his upbringing, so that he bore her imprint of faith in God and regard for the sacred writings of the Old Testament. Mothers today should prayerfully consider the extent of their work with their children in influencing future generations; regardless of financial or time con-

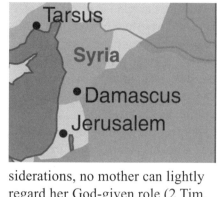

siderations, no mother can lightly regard her God-given role (2 Tim. 1:5; 3:14-15).

His Boyhood in Tarsus

The early years of Saul passed in one of the great Greek cities of the world ("no mean city," Acts 21:39), Tarsus in Cilicia, located near the northeast corner of the Mediterranean Sea. Here East and West met in combining their political, linguistic, and religious influences. The writings and life of Saul provide evidence of such an environment's effect in preparing young Saul for his mission to the Gentile world, but the influence of his spiritual training in youth was stronger (1 Cor. 9:19-23). Here in a center known for its manufacture of cloth from goats' hair, he learned the craft of tent making from his father, who performed his responsibility to train his son in a trade, lest he become a thief. Such training for useful work was associated in the Talmud with making sure the son was circumcised and that he learned the Law. Included with training in the Law would be "the traditions of the fathers."

He spoke both Greek and Hebrew and probably understood Latin, as seen in his steering of his own case through the Roman courts. He also knew something of the public games, which he sometimes employed to stress spiritual purpose and discipline (1 Cor. 9:24ff.; 1 Tim. 4:7-8; 2 Tim. 2:5). While the Hellenistic influence was there in his life, the Hebrew was greater.

Excavations at Tarsus showing a city street. This was the town in which Paul was reared as a child. Photo courtesy of holylandphotos.com

Great Bible Characters: Paul

William Ramsay (*The Cities of St. Paul*, 180) provides evidence of a sizable Jewish settlement in Tarsus, beginning as early as 171 B.C. Both at mother's knee and in the Jewish synagogue he learned about God, the Law of Moses, the divine purpose for Israel, and other matters of spiritual import. His conscience was being formed and molded by spiritual principles, so that he ever tried to do what he believed to be right, though his ignorance was sometimes an impediment (Acts 23:1; 24:16; 1 Tim. 1:12-13). What a monument his life holds to the possibility of rearing children to reverence and serve God in an ungodly environment. In view of his background of preparation to serve and his work among the Gentiles, his separation from birth to be a vessel for carrying the gospel message holds special meaning, especially in his apostolic mission to the Gentiles (Gal. 1:15; Rom. 11:13; Gal. 2:8). Even before he dedicated himself to the sect of the Pharisees, the God of Abraham, Isaac, and Jacob had plans for his life as a spiritual Pharisee.

His Time in History

When we first hear of Saul, he is a young man aiding in Stephen's death (Acts 7:58). In view of customary practice in training the Jewish man for leadership and the sense of "young" in the first century, he could have been thirty to forty years old at the time. Without knowing the definite time, it is easy to understand that his birth could have taken place about the beginning of the Christian Era. It is reasonable to believe that the life of Saul nearly matched that of Jesus and John the Baptist in time, coming possibly five years later. If Stephen died about A.D. 33-35 and Saul died during Nero's persecution close to A.D. 65, then we have approximately thirty years of his life presented in the Acts of the Apostles. What a life he lived for Christ in those prime years of his life.

Whatever religious, political, or cultural influences touched Christians during the first century must also have affected Saul. Judaism (Hebrew religion), Roman citizenship, and Greek culture marked the realm of his life. Though all three of these former influences contributed in some measure to his life, Saul readily gave up all that conflicted with the service of Christ from the time of his conversion, which followed Stephen's death fairly soon.

No date in Saul's life is certain; the dates here used are approximate. The famine of Acts 11 and the accession of Festus to the office of Felix can be respectively placed *close* to A.D. 44 and A.D. 60, though there is some room for difference. His great evangelistic trips most likely occurred between A.D. 44 and 60, leaving his arrest, civil hearings, trip to Rome, and imprisonment—all chronicled in Acts 21-28—to fill out the last five years or so of his life before A.D. 65. From his own pen comes evidence of his elderly status in one of his prison letters, the Letter to Philemon ("Paul the aged," v. 9).

Questions

Define the Following Words in Their Relation to Saul's Life

1. Pharisee: _____

   _____

2. Tarsus: _____

3. Jerusalem: _____

4. Gamaliel: _____

5. Diaspora/Dispersion: _____

Discussion

1. In view of Saul's refusal to glory in his Jewish past, what possible grounds of boasting should Christians today relinquish for the sake of Christ? _____

   _____

2. Why should Christ be the sole ground for the Christian's boasting (glorying), according to 1 Corinthians 1:27-31? _____

3. In view of the many opposing influences, how can parents make sure that their children are consecrated to the service of God?_____

_____

4. To what extent can an individual imbibe influences of the environment in which he lives without compromising his spiritual principles?_____

_____

5. How did Saul's zeal in persecuting the church equip him for preaching the gospel of Christ?_____

_____

6. In what ways did the Lord intend for Saul to serve as an example (1 Tim. 1:16)? _____

_____

7. Give the approximate dates for major events in Saul's life—birth, conversion, missionary journeys, death.

_____

_____

8. In connection with what two events in Saul's life does the New Testament refer to him as "young" and "aged"? _____

_____

9. How did Saul's life as a Pharisee equip him for his work among the Gentiles? What changes did he have to make in attitude to do that work successfully?_____

_____

_____

10. How can parents help their children to form a conscience void of offense toward God and man?_____

_____

_____

11. Is there a lesson to be learned from the Lord's calling Saul to his apostolic office after thirty to forty years of his life? What is it? Consider also Moses' commission to lead Israel out of Egypt at the age of eighty years. Balance this idea against young Timothy's usefulness to Paul. _____

_____

_____

_____

12. Describe Paul's love and concern for his lost kinsmen in the flesh from passages in this lesson. Do you often observe the same love and concern today? _____

_____

_____

Great Bible Characters: Paul

Saul Trains For Leadership in Judaism

The instruction and training that Saul had received in the Old Testament Scriptures at home and in the synagogue were the foundation upon which his later training for leadership in Judaism would rest. Judaism had developed along the lines of the Law of Moses, but there had been numerous additions made to the Law by oral traditions. What began as a divine document had evolved into a human system! The powerful influence of that system is seen in the radical devotion of Saul's life to the Jewish cause and of countless others who were zealously dedicated in similar fashion to the establishment of a material Jewish kingdom under the glorious reign of the Messiah on earth. It will be enlightening to consider the training of Saul.

Passages to Consider

I am indeed a Jew, born in Tarsus of Cilicia, but brought up in this city at the feet of Gamaliel, taught according to the strictness of our fathers' law, and was zealous toward God as you all are today (Acts 22:3, NKJV, as in all references).

But when Paul perceived that one part were Sadducees and the other Pharisees, he cried out in the council, "Men and brethren, I am a Pharisee, the son of a Pharisee; concerning the hope and resurrection of the dead I am being judged! (Acts 23:6).

My manner of life from my youth, which was spent from the beginning among my own nation at Jerusalem, all the Jews know (Acts 26:4).

For you have heard of my former conduct in Judaism, how I persecuted the church of God beyond measure and tried to destroy it. And I advanced in Judaism beyond many of my contemporaries in my own nation, being more exceeding zealous for the traditions of my fathers (Gal. 1:13-14).

. . . circumcised the eighth day, of the stock of Israel, of the tribe of Benjamin, a Hebrew of the Hebrews; concerning the law, a Pharisee; concerning zeal, persecuting the church; concerning the righteousness which is in the law, blameless (Phil. 3:5-6).

Education in the School of Gamaliel

The importance of Saul's training stands out in the first verse as meriting a change of location, so that he might study under the famed

disciples of the Lord. In fact, Saul's opposition to Christianity seemed to be more extreme than that of his teacher, as seen in Gamaliel's moderate approach which he advised the Jewish Council to pursue in Acts 5:34ff. We also see in Acts 23:6 evidence of Saul's training on his faith, in contrast to the skepticism of the Sadducees concerning the hope of the resurrection.

Paul's main concern in the school of Gamaliel was to become as proficient as possible in the

> **Whether the School of Gamaliel approached the level of today's Harvard Divinity School or not, it was traditional Judaism's place to be for an aspiring Pharisee.**

Gamaliel. Whether the School of Gamaliel approached the level of today's Harvard Divinity School or not, it was traditional Judaism's *place to be* for an aspiring Pharisee. It would seem that Saul was studying in Jerusalem during the years of the ministry of Jesus Christ, but we have no actual evidence of his presence or of his seeing Jesus during that time. We do understand his attitude of antipathy toward the Savior from his treatment of the

ancestral traditions of his people. He claimed to have outstripped his contemporaries in the knowledge and practice of the Jewish religion (Gal. 1:14). The way of acceptance with God was obedience to the Law—not only the written Law with its 613 precepts but the oral tradition, transmitted by generations of rabbis and preserved by the School of Hillel, which interpreted those precepts and applied them in detail to every department of contemporary life (F.F. Bruce, *ISBE*, 710).

Saul's approval by his master Gamaliel for the office for which he was being trained certainly propelled him on his persecuting ventures. The boldness of Saul in his persecution of Christians attests the Pharisaic strictness imbued in his training. Another effect of such training was the independence from God exhibited in his pursuit of human religion, because his legal approach to righteousness certainly stood apart from the divine norm of depending upon God for justification: it required his flawless performance of every detail of the Law, both written/divine and oral/human. Robertson (32) says that Saul was "taught to regard the minutest regulation and scruple of the oral tradition as on a par with the very Word of Jehovah." His own assessment was that he was blameless in respect to the Law's righteousness (Phil. 3:5). Within such a context he gained full appreciation of the emptiness of the external ceremonies and the heavy yoke of this approach to the Law. Then he was able and desirous of seeking the righteousness that Jesus Christ provides through his blood (Phil. 3:9).

Evident in the later life of Paul were marks of his training, now being employed in the service of his once arch-enemy, Jesus Christ. His trained mind, skillful use of questions and answers, his practice of dispute with his opponents, his understanding of the strengths and weakness of Phariseeism, though intended to equip him for a career as a rabbi, were actually advantageous to him in his years as a proponent and an apostle of Christ.

> **Integrity is seen in Saul's honest performance of what he thought to be God's will, though he was mistaken in his understanding. Sincerity was a hallmark of his life, for he did it all in good conscience.**

Personal Characteristics

During Saul's years of training, personal characteristics came to the forefront of his personality. His intellectual brilliance and personal ambition later were channeled into a greater cause. While the seeds had been planted during his years of teaching and training at home, it was during the formal training that further cultivation followed. The fruit of the seed and its cultivation in his life was a character marked by integrity, complete devotion, hopeful optimism, and an influence wielded over others. Integrity is seen in Saul's honest performance of what he thought to be God's will, though he was mistaken in his understanding. Sincerity was a hallmark of his life, for he did it all in good conscience (Acts 23:1). He stood up straight and served as he believed best. Devotion is evident in the passionate performance of his task; he never did anything carelessly or halfheartedly. Whatever he did, he did optimistically for the betterment of his cause. Courageous leadership led him to exert his influence for good and against evil, as he saw it. As judged by men, he met the external demands of the Law from a Jewish perspective and was seen as blameless.

Define the Following Words in Their Relation to Saul's Life.

1. Oral tradition: _____

_____

2. Material Jewish Kingdom: _____

3. Hillel: _____

4. Righteousness of the Law: _____

_____

5. Conscience: _____

_____

6. Integrity: _____

Discussion Questions

1. How was the brand of Judaism encountered by Saul different from what the Israelites first met at the giving of

the Law at Mount Sinai? Can you cite some detailed differences? _____

_____

2. What lessons can we learn from the Jewish treatment of the Law and their traditions? _____

_____

3. Why should we honor some kinds of traditions while ignoring others? Which? _____

_____

4. Why do people sometimes exhibit more zeal for human traditions than for divine traditions? Cite some instances of this happening. _____

_____

5. List the passages that teach us of Saul's life as a trainee. _____

_____

6. If Saul was in Jerusalem while Jesus was there, what would have been Saul's attitude toward him? Locate a passage indicating such. _____

7. Contrast the legal righteousness that Saul sought and that which is available under the gospel by faith in Christ. _____

_____

8. How did Saul's attention to the externals of the Law leave him empty and prepare him for the salvation in Jesus Christ? Does this mean that externals make no difference? Give a passage for your answer to his last question. _____

_____

9. Give some of Saul's personal characteristics seen in his life as a persecutor. Did those personal characteristics change when he became a Christian? _____

_____

10. What features of the gospel of Christ should make the Christian optimistic? _____

_____

11. What is the conscience? Discuss the role of conscience in one's efforts to serve God. What are its advantages? Its limitations? Collect all passages dealing with conscience. _____

_____

_____

12. Why does the student/disciple sometimes become more extreme in pursuit of human religion/tradition than his teacher? Consider Jesus' reference to the Pharisees' efforts in proselytizing other Pharisees in Matthew 23:15. _____

_____

_____

Saul's Zeal for Judaism

The foundation of teaching and training that Saul received from his parents and in the synagogue was later expanded in his formal training under Gamaliel. The early part of his life then prepared him mentally, emotionally, and spiritually for the zealous advancement of the cause of Judaism. Like the cannibal who eats without a thought of wrongdoing, he truly believed in its validity and intended to promote it to the glory of God. In doing so he was simply following the dictates of his conscience, based upon the training and education received (Acts 23:1; 24:16). In this regard he illustrates the flaw of depending upon one's conscience as the final arbiter of right.

> **. . .he illustrates the flaw of depending upon one's conscience as the final arbiter of right.**

cution arose against the church which was at Jerusalem; and they were all scattered throughout the regions of Judea and Samaria, except the apostles. And devout men carried Stephen to his burial, and made great lamentation over him. As for Saul, he made havoc of the church, entering every house, and dragging off men and women, committing them to prison. Therefore those who were scattered went everywhere preaching the word (Acts 8:1-4).

Passages to Consider

Then they cried out with a loud voice, stopped their ears, and ran at him with one accord; and they cast him out of the city and stoned him. And the witnesses laid down their clothes at the feet of a young man named Saul (Acts 7:57-58).

Now Saul was consenting to his death. At that time a great perse-

Then Saul, still breathing threats and murder against the disciples of the Lord, went to the high priest (Acts 9:1).

And when the blood of Your martyr Stephen was shed, I also was standing by consenting to his death, and guarding the clothes of those who were killing him (Acts 22:20).

I persecuted this Way to the death, binding and delivering into prisons both men and women, as also the high priest bears me witness, and all the council of the elders, from whom I also received letters to the brethren, and went to Damascus to bring in

chains even those who were there to Jerusalem to be punished (Acts 22:4-5).

So I said, Lord, they know that in every synagogue I imprisoned and beat those who believe on You (Acts 22:19).

Indeed, I myself thought I must do many things contrary to the name of Jesus of Nazareth. This I also did in Jerusalem, and many of the saints I shut up in prison, having received authority from the chief priests; and when they were put to death, I cast my vote against them. And I punished them often in every synagogue and compelled them to blaspheme; and being exceedingly enraged against them, I persecuted them even to foreign cities. While thus occupied, as I journeyed to Damascus with authority and commission from the chief priests (Acts 26:9-12).

For I am the least of the apostles, who am not worthy to be called an apostle, because I persecuted the church of God (1 Cor. 15:9).

For you have heard of my former conduct in Judaism, how I persecuted the church of God beyond measure and tried to destroy it (Gal. 1:13).

. . .although I was formerly a blasphemer, a persecutor, and an insolent man; but I obtained mercy because I did it ignorantly in unbelief (1 Tim. 1:13).

Saul's Persecution of Christians

When we think of Saul's persecution of the Lord's people, we immediately think of some rabid opponent. To some extent this mental picture is probably accurate, but we err in picturing Saul as the narrow Jew of Palestine. A.T. Robertson writes in *The International Standard Bible Encyclopedia* (2276) the following:

He is the Hellenistic Jew, not the Aramaic Jew of Palestine (compare Simon Peter's vision on the house-top at Joppa, for instance). But Paul is not a Hellenizing Jew after the fashion of Jason and Menelaus in the beginning of the Maccabean conflict. Findlay (Hastings, *Dictionary of the Bible* tersely says: "The Jew in him was the foundation of everything that Paul became." But it was not the narrowest type of Judaism in spite of his persecution of the Christians. He belonged to the Judaism of the Dispersion. As a Roman citizen in a Greek city he had departed from the narrowest lines of his people (Ramsay, *Cities of Paul*, 47).

In his Jerusalem training Saul encountered both the strict Judaism and the moderate influence of his teacher. "Paul was fortunate in his great teacher Gamaliel, who was liberal enough to encourage the study of Greek literature" (*ISBE* 2276). In such a combination of influences we can see the making of the man who later became "all things to all men" as he preached "to the Jew first, and also to the Greek" (1 Cor. 9:22; Rom. 1:16).

One should not misconstrue what has been said about Saul's training to mean that he was a "soft" persecutor. No, Luke said that he had ravaged the church of God (Acts 8:3), using a metaphor never again used in the New Testament and based on its literal usage in the Septuagint and classical Greek contexts to describe the uprooting of a vineyard by wild boars. Was the disciple in this case more extreme than his teacher, as sometimes happens? Killing heretics was his way of serving God, only to cause his greater remorsefulness upon the occasion of his conversion. He saw Phariseeism as the world's hope, especially in contrast to Stephen's attacks on much that he held dear (Acts 6:14; 7:48, 52). When Paul later spoke of

giving his consent or voice against the Christians, some even think that he referred to his right to vote as a member of the Jewish Sanhedrin (Acts 26:10).

At the death of Stephen it seems that the Sanhedrin did not even vote, the Romans did not consent, and that Gamaliel did not intervene as in Acts 5; but the Jews took matters into their own hands in a display of mob rule. The young, scholarly rabbi, allowing others to carry out the killing, was there in his zeal silently to encourage the murderers. They probably were trying to give the answer which they could not give to the wise teaching of Stephen on that occasion, but the only answer possible (Acts 6:10).

that he was not a member because of his youth and his not having children. An answer to our question depends on the literal/figurative character of the language used in Acts 26:10. The obvious, natural way to understand it is to construe it literally, in the absence of any contextual clue or linguistic requirement that it be figurative. The argument that he lacked qualification because he was neither old enough nor married depends on later authorities' testimony that such requirements later existed. Saul was certainly familiar with the men making up the Sanhedrin and seemed to represent them (Acts 22:5).

This classic heresy hunter was convinced that Jesus was cursed

> **Killing heretics was his way of serving God, only to cause his greater remorsefulness upon the occasion of his conversion.**

Saul's Leadership in Persecution

After the death of Stephen and the subsequent dispersion of the Christians, Saul moved to the helm of leadership. When we then read of his embarking on a journey to Damascus to arrest Jesus' disciples (Acts 9:1), his very breath reeked of the threats and slaughter he thought to inflict on the church. "The church at Jerusalem"—the unassembled church, the church in a distributive sense—was the object of his attack in Acts 8:1. Both Ananias and the Damascus Christians had heard of his violent exploits (Acts 9:13, 21).

Was young Saul actually part of the Jewish Council? While Saul might not have been a member of the Sanhedrin, he did have a close connection to those leaders. Some have argued that he was; and others,

by God because of his death on the cross (Gal. 3:13), and he thought he had a reasonable basis for his attacks. For this reason and because Jesus opposed the Pharisees, Saul probably made no serious investigation of the claims of Jesus. Would such a great teacher as Gamaliel mislead his stellar student? With this attitude Saul became a champion of orthodox Judaism.

Define the Following Words in Their Relation to Saul's Life.

1. Judaism: _____

2. Sanhedrin:_____

3. Ananias: _____

4. Damascus: _____

5. Unassembled church: _____

Discussion Questions

1. Identify at least five ways in which Saul pursued the persecution of Christians. _____

    _____

    _____

2. List ten different passages where one can learn about Saul the zealous persecutor. _____

    _____

    _____

3. How did Saul consent to the death of Stephen? What can one learn about consenting to evil from the case of Saul?_____

    _____

4. Contrast and compare the different viewpoints of the Hellenistic Jew and the Aramaic/Palestinian Jew. _____

    _____

    _____

    _____

5. Describe the "liberal" and "conservative" influences that had an impact on Saul in his youth. Which influence dominated? _____

    _____

6. Discuss how the persecuting work of Saul ravaged the church. _____

    _____

7. Did "might make right" in the death of Stephen? Prove your answer. _____

    _____

8. Do you conclude that Saul was a member of the Sanhedrin? Why? _____

    _____

9. What factors probably hindered Saul's serious investigation of Jesus' claims? Does this failure of his mean that he was dishonest? _____

    _____

10. Would the Pharisees or the Sadducees be closer to Orthodox Judaism? Give reasons for your answer. _____

    _____

    _____

11. Why do proponents of error often manifest more zeal than proponents of truth? _____

    _____

When Saul was traveling from Jerusalem to Damascus, with his heart set on executing orders from the Jewish Sanhedrin against the disciples of Jesus Christ, little did he think that he soon would be one of those disciples. Those men accompanying him on that famous journey, though we know not their names, would soon witness something that was life-changing to Saul. It would certainly be interesting to know of the futures of those men. Did they also accept the evidence of Jesus Christ and become his followers? Though they might never have become Christians, it is a fact then and now known that "he who formerly persecuted us now preaches the faith which he once sought to destroy" (Gal. 1:23). Many centuries ago Augustine said, "The church owes Paul to the prayer of Stephen" (Conybeare and Howson 62). We should be thankful for the prayer that Stephen prayed and for the God who graciously forgave Saul and gave him to the church for centuries.

Events Surrounding His Conversion

Saul's conversion began as he was journeying from Jerusalem to Damascus to carry out the authority and commission of the high priest to bind and deliver those of "the Way" to Jerusalem. As he drew near to Damascus, light from heaven shined around him, causing him to fall to the ground. The events then following are here presented:

Then he fell to the ground, and heard a voice saying to him, "Saul, Saul, why are you persecuting Me? And he said, "Who are You, Lord?" Then the Lord said, "I am Jesus, whom you are persecuting. It is hard for you to kick against the goads." So he, trembling and astonished, said, "Lord, what do You want me to

Saul's Conversion to Jesus Christ

do?" Then the Lord said to him, "Arise and go into the city, and you will be told what you must do." And the men who journeyed with him stood speechless, hearing a voice but seeing no one. Then Saul arose from the ground, and when his eyes were opened he saw no one. But they led him by the hand and brought him into Damascus. And he was three days without sight, and neither ate nor drank. Now there was a certain disciple at Damascus named Ananias; and to him the Lord said in a vision, "Ananias." And he said, "Here I am, Lord." So the Lord said to him, "Arise and go to the street called Straight, and inquire at the house of Judas for one called Saul of Tarsus, for behold,

he is praying. "And in a vision he has seen a man named Ananias coming in and putting his hand on him, so that he might receive his sight." Then Ananias answered, "Lord, I have heard from many about this man, how much harm he has done to Your saints in Jerusalem. And here he has authority from the chief priests to bind all who call on Your name." But the Lord said to him, "Go, for he is a chosen vessel of Mine to bear My name before Gentiles, kings, and the children of Israel." For I will show him how many things he must suffer for My name's sake." And Ananias went his way and entered the house; and laying his hands on him he said, "Brother Saul, the Lord Jesus,

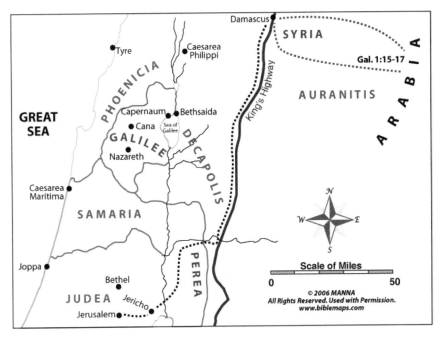

who appeared to you on the road as you came, has sent me that you may receive your sight and be filled with the Holy Spirit." Immediately there fell from his eyes something like scales, and he received his sight at once; and he arose and was baptized. So when he had received food, he was strengthened. Then Saul spent some days with the disciples at Damascus (Acts 9:4-19).

This beginning of Saul's conversion includes the Lord's miraculous appearance from heaven, Ananias' instruction to Saul in the city, and Saul's obedience to that instruction in baptism. Later in this lesson we shall examine the role of the miraculous in the conversion, but there is no denial here of the

sometimes points to the sound, at other times to the import of the words.

- In the city Saul would learn all things appointed for him to do (22:10).

- Ananias, God's messenger to Saul, told him that he needed to stop his praying and to be immersed to wash away his sins, thereby calling on the Lord's name (22:16).

The Supernatural Element in Saul's Conversion

Saul's conversion to Jesus is similar to other cases of conversion recorded in Acts of the Apostles in that it combines both miraculous

version of the others in this group. The purpose of the miracle in Saul's case was to grant this grand character the privilege of seeing Jesus Christ reigning in heaven in order to gain eligibility as a witness of Jesus after his resurrection. His work as an apostle depended upon his being a witness, for his apostleship involved his testifying to what he had seen. Read carefully the two passages following to see that the divine appearance, while a part of Saul's conversion account, did not constitute a crucial element in converting him, but rather in preparing him for his apostolic office.

> Then he said, The God of our fathers has chosen you that you should know His will, and see the Just One, and hear the voice of His mouth. For you will be His witness to all men of what you have seen and heard (Acts 22:14-15).

> But rise and stand on your feet; for I have appeared to you for this purpose, to make you a minister and a witness both of the things which you have seen and of the things which I will yet reveal to you. I will deliver you from the Jewish people, as well as from the Gentiles, to whom I now send you, "to open their eyes, in order to turn them from darkness to light, and from the power of Satan to God, that they may receive forgiveness of sins and an inheritance among those who are sanctified by faith in Me" (Acts 26:16-18).

. . .the vision of the reigning Christ was connected more with his entering the apostolic office than with Saul's conversion to Christ.

need for the ascended and glorified Lord of heaven and earth to confront Saul's unbelief with evidence to move him to belief.

Without quoting the remaining accounts of Saul's conversion from Acts 22 and 26, we note the following significant information from those other accounts of Saul's conversion, because of its supplementary and complementary effect:

- The vision of Jesus occurred about noon (22:6).

- Saul's travel companions saw the light but did not understand the voice of the Lord. This does not mean the sound, but the meaning, as the accusative case of the noun for "voice" shows the verb to mean (22:9).

- All understand that "hear"

and non-miraculous elements. It will be the design of this section to separate the miraculous elements from the non-miraculous and to describe the role of each in his turning to Christ.

Miracle intervened in the life of the belligerent persecutor when the Lord Jesus appeared to him, addressed him, and instructed him to go to Damascus to hear from Ananias. The question of the purpose behind the miracle is legitimate. Perhaps this is a good time to interject that Saul's fellow travelers did not participate in the miracle because they did not see Jesus and did not understand what he was saying. It ought to be manifestly true to any honest reader that, if the miraculous is essential to one's conversion, then the Lord cared not for the con-

The student should observe that the vision of the reigning Christ was connected more with his entering the apostolic office than with Saul's conversion to Christ. While the evidence gained through the vision helped him to confess faith in Jesus as divine, the miracle of the vision was particularly tied to the later work he would do as apostolic witness (cf. Acts 1:8, 21-22). Never did the Lord relate the miraculous vision to his becoming a Christian, a believer, or a saved man. In other cases of conversion the miraculous also played a role, but it never directly contributed to the convert's turning, which occurred apart from means established by the miracle. Twice in the account of the Ethiopian in Acts 8 there was divine appearance to Philip, but never to the convert. In the account of Cornelius in Acts 10, there were three miracles: (1) two involved miraculous appearances to Cornelius and to Peter, to bring the apostle and the sinner together for teaching, and (2) one was the gift of languages to the Gentiles, to persuade the Jews present that God looked on former outcasts as fit subjects of conversion. In the account of the jailer in Philippi in Acts 16, the earthquake, even if a miracle though this is not definite, did not play a direct role in conversion. Let it be noted and remembered that conversion never took place by means of a miracle, in spite of what the popular contention might call for. The conversion of Saul of Tarsus conforms to this principle of truth.

If Saul's conversion did not follow the miraculous route that many claim, then what route did it follow? Those factors that played a crucial role in his turn to the Lord include his hearing the word of the Lord, his belief of the message heard (involving the deity of the reigning Christ), and his willingness to act in obedience to the instructions divinely given. The word spoken to Saul, though first couched in the drapery of a miracle and later non-miraculously spoken by Ananias, sufficiently generated faith in the sinner to move him to obedience to Christ. The next section will pursue this matter more extensively.

Important Questions About Conversion

Perhaps some questions about conversion can help us better to understand the entire matter, especially as it relates to Saul.

1. What is conversion? Conversion is a turning that begins in the mind and culminates in the life. It is based upon the willingness to hear, see, and understand the Lord's word, according to Jesus' reproof of the Jews in Matthew 13:14-16. Though the Calvinist contends that the hearing of the gospel and understanding of it are unnecessary, because the Holy Spirit miraculously provides for such, Jesus said that one must personally perform these functions. He indicates the presence of free will on the part of the sinner; he is not a robot, twisted and turned by the Lord. By his own will he chooses to hear and to turn in his life.

2. Why did Saul need to be converted? For the same reason that all need to be converted—one's own personal sins—Saul also stood in need of conversion. Like the people to whom Peter preached in Acts 3:19, he needed to repent and be converted (turn again), that he might serve the Lord instead of Satan. Just as a person walking in the wrong direction needs to turn around, so the sinner needs to change the direction of his life. Paul expressed this idea in terms of being reconciled to God in 2 Corinthians 5:18-21, implying that the sinner is a spiritual enemy of God because of his own wicked works.

3. What elements are essential to anyone's conversion? In Matthew 13:14-16, we have already learned that each person is free to hear or not hear, see or not see, and understand or not understand. No one is under divine compulsion to react in any certain way. It is also clear in the same passage and in John 6:44-45 that understanding is essential to one's conversion. Jesus makes it clear that teaching/hearing precedes learning, so that the person can come to him, being thereby drawn by the Father. Possibly it is wise to point out that the Father draws; he does not drag any

> . . . it is wise to point out that the Father draws; he does not drag any against his will.

against his will. Because the word of the Lord is what one must hear and learn, then the Bible is essential to conversion (Ps. 19:7-8). No one was ever converted to Christ apart from learning the way of the Lord from the Scriptures. The product of such learning and understanding is obedience from the heart (Rom. 6:17; Heb. 5:9).

4. If conversion involves a change (turning), what changes in the process and what brings about the change? When one honestly hears the gospel, as did every convert in Acts of the Apostles, a change takes place in the *principle* by which he has governed his life, so that the rule of sin is then cancelled (Rom. 10:17; Acts 15:7). Belief (faith), the natural outgrowth of hearing the word of God, then changes his *heart*, canceling his love of sin (Rom. 10:9-10). Repentance, an act of the will to quit sin and start serving the Lord, changes one's *conduct* in canceling his practice of sin (2 Cor. 7:9-11). Baptism, the culminating act of conversion, changes one's *relation* to God by his canceling the guilt of sin. These elements of conversion did not appear in thin air, but they all do appear in the various cases of conversion in Acts.

5. What did Saul give up (sacrifice) in turning to Jesus Christ? Read Philippians 3:4-8 to learn the enormous sacrifice which Saul made. He gave up all that counted in his life in Judaism in order to gain what amounted to nothing in Judaism. On the other hand, viewing it from the divine perspective, he gave up little to gain much more, especially in eternal worth. In 1 Corinthians 4:9-13 Paul described his "miserable" lot, as viewed by men, because of his decision to follow Christ and to serve as his apostle. Pride could have been an obstacle to Saul's conversion and to his apostleship. One who follows Christ today must be willing to renounce all to follow him, even to the point of his very life (Matt. 10:32-39; 19:28-30).

False Ideas Concerning Conversion

Why do many insist that conversion is totally a divine work, in which the human being plays no active part? The notion of man's remaining passive in conversion, so that he is acted upon instead of being the actor, results from a false theory to which many hold. The theory to which we refer is that of *Total Inherited Depravity.* It asserts that each human being since Adam,

except Jesus Christ, has inherited a sinful nature that affects all of the individual's being, so that he can think, speak, or do nothing good without some divine initiative to that end. Total depravity yields total inability. If the theory is true, then no human being can do anything positive toward his salvation; God must first act to initiate the work of conversion.

Without making a lengthy exposé of this theory, we stress one passage already used in this study. In Matthew 18:3 Jesus stated that each human being must be converted and become as a little child; otherwise, there is no entry into the kingdom. Jesus necessarily implied that the child is innocent of sin, not guilty of wrong, when he encouraged all to become like them. Otherwise, he encouraged our becoming worse, not better, to enter the kingdom. Such an absurdity proves that the notion of a child's being born totally depraved is a foolish one. Passages like Psalms 51:5; 58:3; and Ephesians 2:3, employed to prove the theory, are misused, as the context of each reveals.

Another false belief that distorts New Testament teaching about conversion to Christ is the *Faith-only Doctrine.* It holds that because the individual must believe, the Lord bestows the faith as a gift, so that it is not the responsibility of that person. Brief examination of passages teaching the individual to believe demonstrate such a theory to be wrong (John 8:24; Acts 16:31). The use of Ephesians 2:8 to

teach that faith is God's gift misrepresents its meaning; the "it," like "that" earlier in the verse, speaks of the entire idea of being saved by grace through faith in the former part of the verse. We further need to remember that faith is never spoken of as a divine gift, in the sense that the individual has no responsibility for believing.

The following elements, often cited by religious leaders as part of conversion to Christ, are singularly missing from New Testament conversions:

- The presence of a sinful, depraved, or carnal nature

- The necessity of some conversion experience (possibly a vision of Christ or some direct communication from him)

- A confession that God has forgiven one of his sins for Christ's sake

- The sinner's prayer (requesting God to forgive one)

If these elements are truly important in conversion, why are they conspicuously absent from conversions recorded by the hand of inspiration? The New Testament shows that one must hear the gospel of Christ, be mindful of his sins committed (not an inherited sinful nature), repent of his sins, confess faith in Jesus as the Son of God, and be baptized into Christ. Every account of conversion in the Book of Acts shows that hearing the gospel of Christ, usually discounted as unnecessary by most religionists, is the beginning of conversion; no one was ever converted apart from hearing the word taught. The Book of Acts also demonstrates that baptism into Christ was always the culminating act of conversion; apart from baptism no one ever had his sins

> . . .faith is never spoken of as a divine gift, in the sense that the individual has no responsibility for believing.

forgiven. Why do most religious teachers disregard those two parts of conversion always present in the cases of conversion?

Fruits of His Conversion

- When Saul of Tarsus turned to Jesus Christ, he ceased his practice of Judaism. There was no way for him to be a Christian and still remain an adherent of the Mosaic covenant (Rom. 7:1-6). He was willing to turn his back on the religion of his fathers, because he honestly believed Jesus to have risen from the dead and his former religious practice to be contrary to the service of Christ.

- His sacrifice of all that he had formerly held dear in Judaism surely helped him to mature spiritually.

- Joined to Christ, he was then able to bring forth fruit unto God (Rom. 7:4).

- Saul was able to maintain a good conscience, because of his sincere attempt to embrace the right and to cast away the wrong (Acts 23:1).

- Countless souls were harvested by the preaching of the gospel by Paul.

- His own hope of the eternal reward was bright (2 Tim. 4:6-8).

Define These Words in Relation to Their Use in Saul's Life

1. Conversion: _____

2. Augustine: _____

3. The Way: _____

4. Supernatural: _____

5. Witness: _____

6. Calvinist: _____

7. Free will: _____

8. Total Inherited Depravity: _____

9. Faith-only Doctrine: _____

10. Fruits (of conversion): _____

Discussion Questions

1. Explain Augustine's statement: "The church owes Paul to the prayer of Stephen." _____

2. Explain the events surrounding Saul's conversion in their order of occurrence. _____

3. Why do we have three different accounts of his conversion? Where can you find them? _____

4. Why did Jesus personally appear to Saul, but not to the Ethiopian treasurer or to other converts? _____

5. Identify the miraculous elements connected with Saul's conversion. _____

6. Why is Saul the only convert called a witness? _____

7. Is it necessary for people to see a vision of Jesus to be converted? Support your answer with Scripture. _____

_____

8. Contrast what the Calvinist asserts about the sinner's passive role in conversion with what Jesus taught about his active role. _____

_____

_____

9. Why did Saul—sincere, honest, religious man that he was—need to be converted to Christ? _____

_____

10. Compare and contrast some of Saul's sacrifices for the sake of Christ with those that you and others have made in your lifetime. How does humility relate to such sacrifices? _____

_____

_____

11. Explain how Calvinism influences one's view of conversion. What does the Bible teach about this matter? __

_____

_____

12. What evidence is there in Ephesians 2:8 that "it" refers to faith? What evidence is there that "it" refers to one's being saved by grace through faith? _____

_____

13. Explain this statement of Jesus to Saul, in relation to his good conscience: "It is hard for you to kick against the goads." _____

_____

14. Name four parts of conversion, claimed by men as necessary, which do not appear in the Book of Acts. _____

_____

_____

15. What two elements of conversion are always present in the cases of conversion in Acts, which many discount. Why do you think they disregard them? _____

_____

16. Give at least five fruits of Saul's conversion. _____

_____

_____

Saul's Apostleship

Saul's apostleship, initiated by Jesus Christ but doubted by some Judaizers, became the greatest channel of blessing from Christ for the Gentile world. In spite of his apostleship's importance as the centerpiece in the conversion of the pagan world, in the instruction of his fellow Jews, and in the formation of much of the New Testament, there were some who doubted, protested, and denied its validity. While Saul was not one of the original Twelve Apostles chosen by Christ, he did nevertheless receive his apostolic commission from the same Lord, his guidance from the same Spirit, and his credentials from the same King. It will be our aim in this lesson to establish beyond doubt the ground of his apostleship, the qualifications that he held, the powers which he exerted, and the signs that he demonstrated.

Important Passages Relating to His Apostleship

But the Lord said to him, "Go your way, for he is a chosen vessel of Mine to bear My name before Gentiles, kings, and the children of Israel. For I will show him what great things he must suffer for My name's sake" (Acts 9:15-16).

But rise and stand on your feet; for I have appeared to you for this purpose, to make you a minister and a witness both of the things which you have seen and of the things which I will yet reveal to you. I will deliver you from the Jewish people, as well as from the Gentiles, to whom I now send you, to open their eyes, in order to turn them from darkness to light, and from the power of Satan to God, that they may receive forgiveness of sins and an inheritance among those who are sanctified by faith in Me (Acts 26:16-18).

According to the grace of God which was given to me, as a wise master builder I have laid the foundation, and another builds on it. But let each one take heed how he builds on it (1 Cor. 3:10).

For if I preach the gospel, I have nothing to boast of, for necessity is laid upon me; yes, woe is me if I do not preach the gospel! For if I do this willingly, I have a reward; but if against my will, I have been entrusted with a stewardship (1 Cor. 9:16-17).

Then last of all He was seen by me also, as by one born out of due time. For I am the least of the apostles, who am not worthy to be called an apostle, because I persecuted the church of God. But by the grace of God I am what I am, and His grace toward me was not in vain; but I labored more abundantly than they all, yet not I, but the grace of God which was with me (1 Cor. 15:8-10).

Paul, an apostle (not from men nor through man, but through Jesus Christ and God the Father who raised Him from the dead) (Gal. 1:1).

But I make known to you, brethren, that the gospel which was preached by me is not according to man. For I neither received it from man, nor was I taught it, but it came through the revelation of Jesus Christ (Gal. 1:11-12).

But when it pleased God, who separated me from my mother's womb and called me through His grace, to reveal His Son in me, that I might preach Him among the Gentiles, I did not immediately confer with flesh and blood (Gal. 1:15-16).

But on the contrary, when they saw that the gospel for the uncircumcised had been committed to me, as the gospel for the circumcised was to Peter (for He who worked effectively in Peter for the apostleship to the circumcised also worked effectively in me toward the Gentiles) (Gal. 2:7-8).

For this reason I, Paul, the prisoner of Christ Jesus for you Gentiles—if indeed you have heard of the dispensation of the grace of God which was given to me for

> While Saul was not one of the original Twelve Apostles chosen by Christ, he did nevertheless receive his apostolic commission from the same Lord, his guidance from the same Spirit, and his credentials from the same King.

you, how that by revelation He made known to me the mystery (as I have briefly written already, by which, when you read, you may understand my knowledge in the mystery of Christ), which in other ages was not made known to the sons of men, as it has now been revealed by the Spirit to His holy apostles and prophets: that the Gentiles should be fellow heirs, of the same body, and partakers of His promise in Christ through the gospel, of which I became a minister according to the gift of the grace of God given to me by the effective working of His power. To me, who am less than the least of all the saints, this grace was given, that I should preach among the Gentiles the unsearchable riches of Christ, and to make all see what is the fellowship of the mystery, which from the beginning of the ages has been hidden in God who created all things through Jesus Christ (Eph 3:1-9).

And I thank Christ Jesus our Lord who has enabled me, because He counted me faithful, putting me into the ministry, although I was formerly a blasphemer, a persecutor, and an insolent man; but I obtained mercy because I did it ignorantly in unbelief. And the grace of our Lord was exceedingly abundant, with faith and love which are in Christ Jesus. This is a faithful saying and worthy of all acceptance, that Christ Jesus came into the world to save sinners, of whom I am chief. However, for this reason I obtained mercy, that in me first Jesus Christ might show all longsuffering, as a pattern to those who are going to believe on Him for everlasting life (1 Tim. 1:11-16).

Definition of Apostle

The word describing Saul as an apostle—*apostolos*—is no different from that used of other apostles. As a compound noun it derives its

meaning of "one sent out." Other meanings conveyed by the term are delegate, messenger, or one sent with orders (Thayer 68). Because of this broad meaning, the word is variously applied to a variety of kinds of delegates, not just the apostles sent out by Christ.

Both Christ and those not personally sent by him are sometimes referred to as apostles (Heb. 3:1; Acts 14:14; 2 Cor. 8:23). Jesus himself was God's apostle sent from heaven for the work of redemption, while Barnabas and those men-

> In view of such authority from Christ, it should be obvious to all that the words of the apostles, printed in black in the New Testament, are just as weighty and authoritative as the red ones spoken by the Lord himself.

tioned by Paul in his second letter to Corinth were delegates sent out by congregations of the first century on different missions.

Apostolic Authority

The authority of the apostles, including that of Saul, was the authority of Jesus Christ. He specifically promised them roles of authority (twelve thrones, judging) during the time of gospel preaching and conversion (while Jesus sits on his throne, during the regeneration—time of people's new birth into the kingdom) in Matthew 19:28. A similar description of their authority from Christ is found in

Matthew 16:18 and 18:18. In the former passage Jesus spoke to Peter of his role as an apostle, while he addressed all of the apostles in the latter passage. What he gave to Peter (power to bind and loose) in the former, he broadened to all in the latter. Binding and loosing seems to involve their use of the Word of the Lord in ways that would restrict some from entering the spiritual kingdom while allowing others to do so. In John 20:22-23 Jesus anticipated their reception of the Holy Spirit on Pentecost and his guidance of them in teaching the gospel conditions of entrance into the kingdom, thus their remitting or retaining the sins of the hearers. In this apostolic role one assigned and empowered by the King was his ambassador—one fully invested with the King's authority and doing his bidding as his duly authorized representative (2 Cor. 5:20; Eph. 6:20). When sending the Twelve out on a limited mission to the people of Israel and the seventy disciples on a different mission, Jesus similarly placed heaven's authority squarely behind them in Matthew 10:40 and in Luke 10:16: "He who hears you hears Me, he who rejects you rejects Me, and he who rejects Me rejects Him who sent Me."

We shall later learn that Saul shared in this same authority with the other apostles. In demonstration of his authority as being parallel to that of the others, Saul spoke of their all being "stewards of the mysteries of God" (1 Cor. 4:1-2). In this designation he meant those matters once unrevealed during the time of Old Testament dealings, now were given into the keeping and guardianship of the apostles for the purpose of their revelation to the world. To the Galatians he made it clear that it was by revelation of Jesus Christ, not by his conferring with other apostles, that he came to work and speak as an apostle (Gal. 1:1, 11-12, 15-16).

In view of such authority from Christ, it should be obvious to all that the words of the apostles, printed in black in the New Testament, are just as weighty and authoritative as the red ones spoken by the Lord himself. In fact, all of them are equally valuable, true, and authoritative; truly all of them stand out as "red letters." As the next section will show, the writings of Saul are on an equal level of authoritative truth with those of other apostles.

His Commission as an Apostle

That Saul was not one of the original Twelve Apostles, chosen and trained by the Lord himself for their work after his ascension, is clear to any student of the New Testament. His was an "untimely birth" in relation to his commission as an apostle, in the sense of his becoming a witness later than the other apostles and by a different means. Jesus was still present on earth at the time of the calling and qualifying of the Twelve, but he appeared miraculously to Saul to qualify him. How then does he fit into the picture? The Lord also selected him "last of all," meaning "finally," thereby qualifying him as a witness of the resurrected Christ, and commissioned him to the apostolic office. In spite of his special and different call and qualification, he did not rank behind the other apostles (2 Cor. 11:5). The nature of the qualification of Saul and the other apostles forbids any line of apostolic succession to follow after the New Testament apostles, in spite of the claim of some religious groups (Roman Catholic, Church of England/Episcopalian) that their

"bishops" are successors to the apostles.

In Acts 9 and Acts 26, quoted in an earlier section of this lesson, the appearance of Jesus to Saul during his travel to Damascus is set forth. His vision of the risen Christ, while producing belief in Saul so that he could turn to Jesus Christ, was primarily related to his becoming an apostolic witness. There the Lord told Saul of his purpose for him as a minister (servant) and a witness, and he assured him of an adequate foundation for any testimony he would give to Jews, Gentiles, and kings through past and future revelations that he would grant to him. Even to

> . . .the writings of Saul are on an equal level of authoritative truth with those of other apostles.

Ananias the Lord gave assurance of Saul's status as a chosen vessel. Later Paul spoke of his being a master builder who had worked on the foundation of the church in Corinth (1 Cor. 3:10), even as other apostles and prophets labored similarly on the foundation of the Lord's church (Eph. 2:20). Later references to his apostleship as not resting upon men or conferred by other apostles can be more readily understood against the background of problems raised by his enemies about the validity of his apostleship. The grace of being chosen to serve as an apostle, not the grace bringing salvation, seems to be the meaning in passages like Ephesians 3:2 and 1 Timothy 1:14. Because of his violent opposition to Christ and his followers, he ever felt keenly his unworthiness to be in such a role in the spread of the gospel of the kingdom.

The Signs of His Apostleship

From the reliable testimony of the inspired Scriptures we learn much about the qualification, call, commission, inspiration, and authority of Saul for the apostleship. Those of the first century did not have our advantage in reading all of these various passages in the New Testament Scriptures. They had to discern his apostleship from the signs given to him in proof of the office. "Truly the signs of an apostle were accomplished among you with all perseverance, in signs and wonders and mighty deeds" (2 Cor. 12:12). Not only does Paul here write of his signs of apostleship, but he also indicated what such signs were. They consisted of signs

(*sēmeion*), wonders (*teras*), and powers/mighty deeds (*dunamis*). A.T. Robertson's *Word Pictures in the New Testament* (V, 343) says that these words, in order, signify God's purpose in the miracles, God's attracting attention, and God's power or energy. In the case of Paul's use of such signs, God was attracting attention by means of the miracles energized by God to the words spoken by the apostle as divinely given words. He was calling attention to the truth of the message by directing attention to the messenger as one sent by God and speaking for God. Other passages which speak of such signs are Romans 15:18-19 and Hebrews 2:4.

All claiming to be present-day apostles or successors to the apostles, including the Mormon apostles and others, are obligated to demonstrate their apostleship by the same signs of the early apostles. If they possess the right to be recognized as apostles, then we have the right to request and expect their signs to be displayed. In reality they claim an office no longer existing and a power no more exerted. They would replace the apostles selected by Christ, who were acknowledged by him as occupying their thrones through the time of the regeneration of the gospel dispensation, with men merely claiming to be apostles. They are no more apostles than some claiming to be Christ are the true Christ. Anybody can claim, but none can verify the claim by showing the signs of an apostle. In the congregation at Ephesus there had been a situation of some falsely claiming to be apostles (Rev. 2:2). The church had tested them, probably by demanding them to demonstrate their signs, but the lying men had failed the test. It is also possible that some in the church used the miraculous gift of discernment to determine that the false apostles were lying (1 Cor. 12:10). Whatever the test applied at Ephesus, we still have an adequate means of testing any claiming to be apostles, just as we have the divine standard of truth for testing any message taught by any person claiming to be from God. It is in this access to the apostolic teaching of the first century that we still have the apostles chosen by Jesus. They are still serving as the world's teachers, just as the Lord meant for them to do when he assigned them this role in Matthew 19:28.

Define These Words in Relation to Their Use in Saul's Life

1. Apostle: _____

2. Regeneration: _____

3. Binding and loosing: _____

4. Stewards of the mysteries of God: _____

5. One born out of due time: _____

6. Apostolic succession: _____
   _____

7. Chosen vessel: _____

8. Signs of an apostle: _____

9. Signs, wonders, and mighty deeds (powers in some versions): _____
   _____

10. Gift of discernment: _____

Discussion Questions

1. Relate Saul's call to be an apostle in your own words. _____
   _____
   _____

2. Cite three areas in which the importance of Saul's apostleship stands out as the centerpiece. _____
   _____
   _____

3. Though Saul was not one of the original twelve apostles, he did enjoy three advantages in common with them. Name them. _____
   _____

4. Name the three groups to whom Jesus said he would send Saul. _____
   _____

5. Paul once wrote about his being the last apostle. Cite the passage and explain what he said. _____

_____

6. Cite instances of others than the apostles of Christ being called apostles and explain the meaning in those passages. _____

_____

7. What did Paul mean in referring to himself as an ambassador of Christ? Relate his role as ambassador to the King sending him, the authority given him, and the credentials provided him. _____

_____

8. Why are Paul's writings equally authoritative with those of other apostles or the teachings of Jesus Christ?

_____

_____

9. Explain the following passages in connection with Paul's apostleship: 1 Corinthians 3:10; Ephesians 2:29; 3:1; 1 Timothy 1:14. _____

_____

_____

10. How could first-century Christians be sure about a man's apostleship? Cite passages and specific cases.

_____

_____

11. How can we test modern-day "apostles"? _____

_____

12. In what sense do we still have the apostles on their thrones in their role of judging? _____

_____

_____

Early Travels of the New Convert

There was no stopping the young Saul, who had recently seen the resurrected Christ and been called by him to take the gospel to the world. Much that had happened to Saul in his practice of Judaism had prepared him for this new work, though the message he would proclaim was an unexpected one from his earlier perspective. Parents, religious leaders, Gama-

by any means I may attain to the resurrection of the dead (Phil. 3:10-11).

As he ever tried to understand something of the teachings, deeds, attitude, example, priorities, values, and mission of the risen Christ, he more and more emulated his Lord and Master, being empowered by his resurrection from the dead to a discipleship never before seen

> **His zeal was observable early in his travels, even in the ten to twelve years from his conversion to his First Missionary Journey.**

liel, encouragement of fellow Jews, and much more had formed in him the kind of man whom the Lord could use. The very vision of the Damascus Road, with its focus on one whom he had earlier denied but now confessed, would continue to supply the spiritual fuel that would keep him going. At the center of that focus was the fact, the reality, of Jesus' resurrection from the dead; Saul constantly sought to know the power of his resurrection.

. . .that I may know him and the power of his resurrection, and the fellowship of his suffering, being conformed to his death, if

or since displayed. His zeal was observable early in his travels, even in the ten to twelve years from his conversion to his First Missionary Journey.

An Auspicious Beginning in Damascus

Then Saul arose from the ground, and when his eyes were opened he saw no one. But they led him by the hand and brought him into Damascus. And he was three days without sight, and neither ate nor drank. Now there was a certain disciple at Damascus named Ananias; and to him the Lord said in a vision, "Ananias." And he said,

"Here I am, Lord." So the Lord said to him, "Arise and go to the street called Straight, and inquire at the house of Judas for one called Saul of Tarsus, for behold, he is praying. And in a vision he has seen a man named Ananias coming in and putting his hand on him, so that he might receive his sight. Then Ananias answered, "Lord, I have heard from many about this man, how much harm he has done to Your saints in Jerusalem. And here he has authority from the chief priests to bind all who call on Your name." But the Lord said to him, "Go, for he is a chosen vessel of Mine to bear My name before Gentiles, kings, and the children of Israel. For I will show him how many things he must suffer for My name's sake." And Ananias went his way and entered the house; and laying his hands on him he said, "Brother Saul, the Lord Jesus, who appeared to you on the road as you came, has sent me that you may receive your sight and be filled with the Holy Spirit." Immediately there fell from his eyes something like scales, and he received his sight at once; and he arose and was baptized. So when he had received food, he was strengthened. Then Saul spent some days with the disciples at Damascus. Immediately he preached the Christ in the synagogues, that He is the Son of God. Then all who heard were amazed, and said, "Is this not he who destroyed those who called on this name in Jerusalem, and has come here for that purpose, so that he might bring them bound to the chief priests?" But Saul increased all the more in strength, and confounded the Jews who dwelt in Damascus, proving that this Jesus is the Christ (Acts 9:8-22).

"Therefore, King Agrippa, I was not disobedient to the heavenly vision, but declared first to those in Damascus and in Jerusalem, and throughout all the region of

Judea, and then to the Gentiles, that they should repent, turn to God, and do works befitting repentance. For these reasons the Jews seized me in the temple and tried to kill me. Therefore, having obtained help from God, to this day I stand, witnessing both to small and great, saying no other things than those which the prophets and Moses said would come—that the Christ would suffer, that He would be the first to rise from the dead, and would proclaim light to the Jewish people and to the Gentiles." Now as he thus made his defense, Festus said with a loud voice, "Paul, you are beside yourself! Much learning is driving you mad!" But he said, "I am not mad, most noble Festus, but speak the words of truth and reason" (Acts 26:19-25).

When blind Saul entered Damascus, little did he or anyone else expect him soon to be turning spiritually blind people to the light of Jesus Christ, and that in the town where he had ended his work of persecuting Christians. Saul's zeal in opposing Christ was quickly converted to advancing his cause, indicating the powerful impact of his vision of the resurrected Lord. Days spent with the disciples in Damascus soon turned into proclamation of Christ's deity in the town's synagogues. Those Jews hearing him, knowledgeable of his purpose for coming to Damascus, were troubled and confused by his putting together proofs that Jesus was the Christ (Messiah) foretold by the prophets and sent by the Father. Such uproar caused by his teaching provided Saul an opportune time to leave for solitude elsewhere.

Let us note that Saul did not spend endless time in confusion or dismay after his conversion to Christ. Understanding that his purpose in life was to serve Christ,

he began to "bloom where he was planted." Each one can "brighten the corner where you are." Like Saul, we have been saved to serve and ought to waste no time in doing what we can wherever we can and whenever we can. Appointment by an elder or a request by a mature Christian to do something is not necessary for one who has been enlisted to serve by our Royal Commander.

> There is much to do;
> there's work on every hand.
> Hark! the cry for help comes
> ringing through the land.
> Jesus calls for reapers;
> I must active be.
> What wilt thou, O Master?
> Here am I, send me.
> (M.W. Spencer)

let him down through the wall in a large basket (Acts 9:23-25).

In Damascus the governor, under Aretas the king, was guarding the city of the Damascenes with a garrison, desiring to arrest me; but I was let down in a basket through a window in the wall, and escaped from his hands (2 Cor. 11:32-33).

In Galatians 1:18 Paul says that three years passed from his conversion to his trip to Jerusalem, probably to reinforce his lack of dependence on the other apostles or any other humans ("flesh and blood"), for he did not even see the other apostles for those years. His apostleship did not depend on their appointment or instruction, but on Christ's appearance and commission. Those three years,

Like Saul, we have been saved to serve and ought to waste no time in doing what we can wherever we can and whenever we can.

Retreat to Arabia and Return to Damascus

But when it pleased God, who separated me from my mother's womb and called me through His grace, to reveal His Son in me, that I might preach Him among the Gentiles, I did not immediately confer with flesh and blood, nor did I go up to Jerusalem to those who were apostles before me; but I went to Arabia, and returned again to Damascus. Then after three years I went up to Jerusalem to see Peter, and remained with him fifteen days (Gal.1:15-18).

Now after many days were past, the Jews plotted to kill him. But their plot became known to Saul. And they watched the gates day and night, to kill him. Then the disciples took him by night and

"many days" in Acts 9:23 evidently marked his stay in Arabia (which fits between 9:22 and 9:23, in my judgment), left him time to retire for reflection and spiritual preparation for the great work that he would soon begin. It is possible that he taught the gospel to people while there; but Luke gives no such information about people whom Saul converted, churches which he began, any accomplishment that he made, or even the trip itself. Because such information is the usual order in Luke's narrative, it seems reasonable to conclude that such was not Saul's real purpose in Arabia.

Arabia in the first century A.D. extended from the area just east of Damascus all the way to Sinai in the South (Gal. 4:24), leaving Saul much room to travel. Several writers have conjectured that he went five hundred to six hundred miles to Sinai (about and there meditated on the difference between the Law of Moses and Justification by Faith, but such an idea is truly more the offspring of doctrinal presupposition than of factual information). It is probably more reasonable to think of his travel to the closer region of Arabia, located only approximately seventy-five miles to the east or southeast.

After some time, Saul came back to the city of his conversion, where he then became the object of persecution by those with whom he once collaborated ("Chickens come home to roost"). Their opposition grew so fierce that the local Christians, acting in concert with Saul, aided his escape. The enemies of the apostle had enlisted the help of the governor in guarding the gates around the clock, necessitating an exit at night. Otherwise, an exceedingly fruitful ministry would have been aborted much too early. Where would the rejected (but not dejected) apostle now go?

Eventually to Jerusalem

And when Saul had come to Jerusalem, he tried to join the disciples; but they were all afraid of him, and did not believe that he was a disciple. But Barnabas took him and brought him to the apostles. And he declared to them how he had seen the Lord on the road, and that He had spoken to him, and how he had preached boldly at Damascus in the name of Jesus. So he was with them at Jerusalem, coming in and going out. And he spoke boldly in the name of the Lord Jesus and disputed against the Hellenists, but they attempted to kill him (Acts 9:26-29).

Now it happened, when I returned to Jerusalem and was

> He undoubtedly received from him and James, the Lord's brother, much help in the form of encouragement and information about their labors, but his revelation came directly from the Lord

praying in the temple, that I was in a trance and saw Him saying to me, "Make haste and get out of Jerusalem quickly, for they will not receive your testimony concerning Me." So I said, "Lord, they know that in every synagogue I imprisoned and beat those who believe on You. And when the blood of Your martyr Stephen was shed, I also was standing by consenting to his death, and guarding the clothes of those who were killing him." Then He said to me, "Depart, for I will send you far from here to the Gentiles" (Acts 22:17-21).

. . .nor did I go up to Jerusalem to those who were apostles before me; but I went to Arabia, and returned again to Damascus. Then after three years I went up to Jerusalem to see Peter, and remained with him fifteen days. But I saw none of the other apostles except James, the Lord's brother. (Now concerning the things which I write to you, indeed, before God, I do not lie) (Gal. 1:17-20).

Whether Saul felt rejected and dejected upon his initial attempt to become part of the Jerusalem group of disciples or not, we do not know; but from a human perspective he certainly had reason to feel that way, after such hostile treatment in Damascus and suspicious treat-

ment by brethren in Damascus. For him Barnabas was a "savior." Every congregation needs a "Barnabas," one who can discern the value and anticipate the potential of people cast aside like Saul. Barnabas had already proved himself both generous and encouraging/consoling in earlier dealings with the Jerusalem church (Acts 4:36-37). In this present instance he took Saul to the apostles and made a courageous defense of the new convert by explaining his vision of Christ, call by Christ, and bold stand in Damascus. Thereby he achieved acceptance of Saul by the church, so that he participated fully in daily fellowship and work. It seems almost uncanny that Saul then—after passing on this trip the location of his vision on the trip to Damascus—exhibited his former boldness in Jerusalem, probably strengthened by Barnabas' heroics boldness, in defense of his former enemy. Did he work for Christ in some of the same Hellenist synagogues (where Greek-speaking Jews gathered) where he had fought him? While we do not know, the possibility is intriguing, as he sought to undo some of his former damage done to the cause of the Lord.

Why had Saul come to Jerusalem? We know it was not to receive the endorsement of Peter or the approval of the original apostles, though he did hope to spend time with Peter—some two weeks he tells us. He undoubtedly received from him and James, the Lord's brother, much help in the form of encouragement and information about their labors, but his revelation came directly from the Lord (Gal. 1:11-12). He also had opportunity to demonstrate his commitment to Christ, which was so clear that the obstinate Jews tried to kill Saul. The Lord then revealed to him in ecstatic vision (*ekstasis*) that he should leave the city and go to teach Gentiles. Other apostles, unmentioned as being present, evidently were elsewhere when Saul was in Jerusalem, unless one thinks he deliberately avoided them.

To Caesarea and Then to Tarsus

And he spoke boldly in the name of the Lord Jesus and disputed against the Hellenists, but they attempted to kill him. When the brethren found out, they brought him down to Caesarea and sent him out to Tarsus (Acts 9:29-30).

Afterward I went into the regions of Syria and Cilicia. And I was unknown by face to the churches of Judea which were in Christ. But they were hearing only, "He who formerly persecuted us now preaches the faith which he once tried to destroy." And they glorified God in me (Gal. 1:21-24).

Saul's disputing with the Hellenists required his leaving and going to Caesarea, where he apparently took a ship for this trip of some four hundred miles to the region of his homeland. Having associated only with those Christians in Jerusalem, he was still personally unknown to brethren elsewhere in Judea, though they heard about his preaching the faith of Jesus Christ during this trip to the north. He was able to spend time in Tarsus for the first time, perhaps, in a number of years.

Were the elderly parents of Paul still living? How had they reacted toward his turn to Jesus Christ? Had they also turned to him? What reception did they give to their son, whom they knew to be a man of sincerity and honesty? These questions will remain unanswered in our study, in order not to speculate about them; but they surely pique our interest.

It is significant that this tireless worker willingly toiled in the harvest field seeking souls for Christ

> So great was the harvest of souls that Barnabas saw the need for a helper prepared to rise to this Gentile challenge; he chose his former associate from Jerusalem, Saul of Tarsus.

among the people of his home region. There were certainly opportunities to teach Gentiles, as the Lord had meant for him to do. If a man seeks the endorsement/support of his brethren for work abroad, it is always wise to inquire about his work at home. Some have placed his "visions and revelations" in 2 Corinthians 12:1-10 at Tarsus during this trip, though their time and place are uncertain, being placed by others in Antioch later in Acts 11. Wherever and whenever Saul received them, he also received what he needed to encourage his humility for the work that lay ahead of him.

Helping Barnabas in Antioch

Now those who were scattered after the persecution that arose over Stephen traveled as far as Phoenicia, Cyprus, and Antioch, preaching the word to no one but the Jews only. But some of them were men from Cyprus and Cyrene, who, when they had come to Antioch, spoke to the Hellenists, preaching the Lord Jesus. And the hand of the Lord was with them, and a great number believed and turned to the Lord. Then news of these things came to the ears of the church in Jerusalem, and they sent out

Barnabas to go as far as Antioch. When he came and had seen the grace of God, he was glad, and encouraged them all that with purpose of heart they should continue with the Lord. For he was a good man, full of the Holy Spirit and of faith. And a great many people were added to the Lord. Then Barnabas departed for Tarsus to seek Saul. And when he had found him, he brought him to Antioch. So it was that for a whole year they assembled with the church and taught a great many people. And the disciples were first called Christians in Antioch. (Acts 11:19-26).

Jewish Christians who had left Jerusalem upon the intensifying persecution are the ones here mentioned as beginning to preach to Greeks (hellēnistas), after their earlier efforts to teach Jews. In their first mission to Gentiles some from Cyprus and Cyrene met with much success. It is interesting to note that no apostle had a part in starting this new Gentile church; evidently the brethren saw no need for the apostles' help, as they themselves were growing more self-reliant in their capacity to work with the Lord's help in such matters. Upon receiving word of this great development, saints in Jerusalem dispatched Barnabas, himself from Cyprus and well qualified for this task, to encourage and enlarge the work of salvation by grace. He had earlier demonstrated his wisdom and carefulness in the Lord's work with Saul in Jerusalem. So great was the harvest of souls that Barnabas saw the need for a helper prepared to rise to this Gentile challenge; he chose his former associate from Jerusalem, Saul of Tarsus. Saul had been preparing for such a task all of his life. Even recently in Jerusalem and Tarsus he had been preparing to work among Gentiles and Jews. Now he and Barnabas formed a

vital team working for a year to encourage the saved and to enlist new disciples. In this first Gentile congregation, in whose formation no apostle had played a part, the Lord called the disciples Christians for the first time. While some have contended that enemies first derisively hurled the new name to the disciples, no such evidence exists; and much evidence—in the other eight New Testament occurrences of the verb (chrēmatizo)—shows that it universally denoted something that God did.

Mission of Mercy to Jerusalem

And in these days prophets came from Jerusalem to Antioch. Then one of them, named Agabus, stood up and showed by the Spirit that there was going to be a great famine throughout all the world, which also happened in the days of Claudius Caesar. Then the disciples, each according to his ability, determined to send relief to the brethren dwelling in Judea. This they also did, and sent it to the elders by the hands of Barnabas and Saul (Acts 11:27-30).

And Barnabas and Saul returned from Jerusalem when they had fulfilled their ministry, and they also took with them John whose surname was Mark (Acts 12:25).

A prophet named Agabus, in the company of other prophets who had come to Antioch from the Christians in Jerusalem, prophesied the coming of a famine through the Roman world (probably the meaning, as in Luke 2:1) during the reign of Claudius (A.D. 41-54). An ancient historian named Eusebius recorded in his *Ecclesiastical History* (57-58) that such a famine took place. In fact, historians tell us of other famines in Egypt and Syria with their empire-wide effects. There is no reason to doubt the veracity of this prophecy,

which seems to have taken place between A.D. 44 and 47. During this time of anticipated need, Christians in Antioch compassionately decided to send relief to their Judean brethren, who evidently needed assistance at other times in the future, according to the New Testament record, possibly because of persecution aimed at them (Rom. 15:25-26; 1 Cor. 16:1-3; 2 Cor. 8-9; Heb. 10:32-34). Their free-will offering of their means to aid the brethren is typical of Christians in the first century, but in this instance Gentile people were helping their Jewish brethren. What a model of the spirit of sharing!

Barnabas and Saul were the emissaries of the church in taking the relief to the elders in Judea, wherever they worked and oversaw local churches. The stupendous claim made by those with an agenda to support a centralized organizational scheme unknown to the New Testament—that Jerusalem elders served as sponsoring-church elders to oversee the distribution of the relief funds—has no support whatever in the Scriptures. The elders, here mentioned first in Acts, worked in and oversaw the different churches. To extend their operation and oversight lacks authority and conflicts with restrictions in 1 Peter 5:1-4. The relief was sent to other congregations to enable them to help their needy members.

When Barnabas and Saul had completed their mission on this trip of close to six hundred miles, they returned to Antioch with John Mark, who would later travel with them on the first of three long evangelistic trips. Saul's early travels, studied in this lesson, were a mere warm-up for greater work through much of the Roman Empire.

Define These Words as Used in Relation to Their Use in Saul's Life

1. Power of his resurrection: _____

2. Three years (Gal. 1:18): _____

3. Flesh and blood (Gal. 1:16): _____

4. Arabia: _____

5. Son of Encouragement (Acts 4:36-37): _____

6. Hellenist: _____

7. Trance: _____

8. Greeks: _____

9. Famine: _____

10. Sponsoring-church plan: _____

11. John Mark: _____

Discussion Questions

1. Identify and discuss the various people or influences which had prepared Saul for the work that he was here beginning. _____

    _____

    _____

2. Discuss how the resurrection of Jesus must have impacted Saul during his work for Christ. _____

    _____

3. What are some of the ironies of Saul's beginning his work in Damascus? _____

    _____

4. What important lesson do we learn from Saul's beginning to work for the Lord where he was? _____

    _____

5. What were the possible destinations of Saul in his trip to Arabia? Is there one part that seems more reasonable to you than the others? _____

    _____

6. To what end did the Jews of Damascus go in an effort to stop Saul's work? To what ends do enemies of the gospel go today for the same purpose? _____

    _____

7. What role did Barnabas play early after Saul's conversion? Why does each congregation need a Barnabas?

    _____

    _____

    _____

8. What evidence do you see in this lesson that Peter was not a pope? _____

    _____

9. Why did Saul receive visions and revelations? Why did the Lord permit his thorn in the flesh? _____

_____

_____

10. In view of the starting of the Antioch church without the help of an apostle, it might be good to discuss whether each new congregation needs a preacher for them to start working for the Lord. What are the essentials for starting such a work? _____

_____

_____

11. By consulting a concordance giving such information, someone could find the passages where "called" is used in the New Testament and help the class to learn that it always expresses something done by God.

_____

_____

12. What can you learn about the local church's work of relieving needy saints in other congregations? _____

_____

_____

13. What is unusual about this case of benevolent help? What can we learn from this unusual aspect of the case?

_____

_____

_____

14. What is the role of elders in the work of the church? How far does their oversight extend? How is this principle violated in the sponsoring-church plan? _____

_____

_____

_____

Paul Travels The World For Christ (1)

Though recently converted, Saul soon began a rigorous effort to spread the word of Christ to the benighted residents of earth, in obedience to the call of the Lord in miraculous vision. His frequent travels, referred to by him in 2 Corinthians 11:26 as part of his surpassing work for Christ, would now begin to encompass trips to all parts of the Roman world. In addition to the miles covered, there were also additional hardships encountered on these journeys, which he also mentioned (2 Cor. 11:23-33). Such were the struggles that he endured for the Lord and his cause. In this lesson we begin to make our way through his various travels that took him through the Roman Empire.

Saul's first journey would take him, Barnabas ("Son of Consolation" and a Levite, Acts 4:36), and John Mark (son of Mary and cousin of Barnabas, Acts 12:12; Col. 4:10) from Syrian Antioch westward to Cyprus and then north to Asia Minor on a trip of some 1,200 miles to spread the word of Christ to Jews and to Gentiles during the next two years (approximately A.D. 45-47). The student should read Acts 13 and 14 while studying this material.

The circumstances surrounding the beginning of this first journey are somewhat unusual. Barnabas and Saul are mentioned by Luke among the prophets and teachers in the Antioch church. As these men were serving and fasting, the Spirit of God gave revelation concerning their leaving on this trip. "Separate to me Barnabas and Saul for the work to which I have called them" (Acts 13:2). Remember that God had already in purpose separated

Antioch of Syria is known as Antayka. Photo courtesy of HolylandPhotos.org.

Saul from his mother's womb and that Christ had already called him (Gal. 1:15; Acts 26:15-18). The Holy Spirit was here echoing his earlier divine call and mission. Prayer, fasting, and laying on of hands by the other prophets and teachers surely involved their supplication to God for his blessing in a time of serious reflection on the serious mission that lay ahead and the brethren's expressed approval of the two for the work. With their blessings, prayers, and support they sent them forward, the Holy Spirit concurring.

With Antioch of Syria as their point of departure, this journey included the following stops:

1. Seleucia: It seems that this town was their port for embarking on this first journey, with no mention of teaching here. It was situated just north of the Orontes River and sixteen miles to the southwest of the metropolis of Antioch (some distances cited in Saul's journeys are those found in *Baker's Bible Atlas;* others are estimated by the author).

Cyprus

This island lay some sixty miles west of Syria and forty miles south of Asia Minor. Saul and Barnabas, a native of Cyprus, made two stops on this island.

2. Salamis: Located on the eastern end of Cyprus, synagogues of the Jews (indicating a sizable Jewish population) provided an audience to hear them proclaiming the word. We know nothing about

the results of the teaching. Note that Saul's first attempt was to teach the Jews at his different stops. John Mark was described as their assistant, providing whatever help they needed.

3. Paphos: Luke seems to mean that they traveled by land ("gone through the island to Paphos") to reach this city on the western end of Cyprus, some ninety miles away. Luke says nothing of their teaching along the way, but he does record their notable success with Sergius Paulus.

This proconsul was an official chosen by the Roman Senate to oversee a senatorial province, in contrast to a legate who oversaw an imperial province after his appointment by the emperor. Bible critics once thought Luke mistaken in referring to a proconsul assigned to Cyprus, because they thought it was an imperial province. Archaeology has demonstrated their mistake and Luke's accuracy, because what

Perga. The two, partially preserved, circular towers guard the southern entrance to Perge. They were built in the third century B.C. and were standing when Paul, Barnabas, and John Mark visited the city about A.D. 47. The twin towers still stand to a height of almost 40 feet [12 m.]! A Roman era agora is visible to the right (east) of the gate as is the beginning of a 980 foot [300 m.] long street leads north from this gate. On the horizon on the left side of the image is the flat–topped acropolis of Perge. Photo and caption courtesy of HolylandPhotos.org.

was once an imperial province later became a senatorial province about twenty years before Christ's birth. In fact, near Paphos a Roman inscription bearing Paulus' name as proconsul confirms Luke's preciseness (Keller 383).

Sergius Paulus' desire to hear the teaching of God's men was initially thwarted by a local Jewish false prophet and sorcerer named Elymas or Bar-Jesus. After Paul's rebuke of the opponent of right (note the change of Saul's name at this point in the inspired record, as reflected in the title of this lesson and later references), he then miraculously made him blind and left him in a miserable state. Having seen the miracle and astonished at the Lord's teaching, the proconsul then believed.

Asia Minor

4. Perga in Pamphylia: To reach the mainland from Cyprus, the travel party had to sail 170 miles to the northwest, probably landing at Attalia, on their way to Perga, twelve miles inland. John Mark left Paul and Barnabas at this point, for some unrecorded reason. We do learn later that Paul did not wish to travel with Mark on the second journey, because of this incident (Acts 15:36-41); but he later described him useful for service (2 Tim. 4:11). One major obstacle to the religion of Christ here was the worship of Artemis (Diana), though Luke does not mention it. As in other centers of pagan idolatry, sensuous ceremonies characterized such practice and held much fleshly appeal to those looking for something to satisfy the outward person.

5. Antioch in Pisidia: Paul went first to the synagogue on the Sabbath, where he used the opportunity offered to speak to the

The fertility goddess Diana was worshiped throughout Asia.

Jews and "God-fearers" (probably uncircumcised Gentiles who worshiped Jehovah without full conversion to Judaism, same as "devout proselytes" in v. 43; cf. Acts 10:2, 22; 13:26) about God's purpose in working with Israel to bring the Messiah to earth, so that all could escape their sins through faith in Jesus. It is amazing that his discourse was so similar to that of Stephen, which had aroused the harsh opposition of Saul and other Jews in Acts 7. Notice the brief outline of the sermon:

A. God's choice of the patriarchs, exaltation of the people in Egypt, leading them in the Exodus, sustaining them in the wilderness forty years, giving them their land inheritance in Canaan for about 450 years, and giving them judges until Samuel (13:17-20).

B. The people's rebellious request for a king and the divine permission of Saul and David (13:21-22).

C. God's sending of a Savior in Jesus Christ, David's seed, attested by John the Immerser (13:23-25).

D. Jewish resistance to Jesus and murder of him sent by God, in ignorance of their prophets (13:26-29).

E. God's raising of Jesus from the tomb and showing of him to witnesses, who later declared the "word of this salvation" (v. 26) and warned about their repudiation of Jesus (13:30-41).

The hearers asked for another opportunity to hear this message on the next Sabbath. When the Jews (possibly leaders) saw the huge crowd gathered, they enviously contradicted the teaching and blasphemed. Jewish resistance provided the preachers the opportunity to teach Gentiles, among whom there were many disposed ("appointed" by God's plan and their willingness, v. 48) to hear the word, believe, and obey it. Again there was Jewish opposition, even to the point of running Paul and Barnabas out of town. The rejected preachers then figuratively rejected these people who had rejected the apostolic word, but they left behind new disciples who were filled with joy and with the Holy Spirit.

6. Iconium: Again the travelers went to the synagogue to teach Jews and Greeks, a great number of whom believed; but disbelieving Jews succeeded in poisoning the minds of the Gentiles against the brethren. In spite of the Lord's granting miracles to be done by them, most of the people there were divided. Paul and Barnabas had to flee to their next stop when the opponents tried to stone them.

Lycaonia

7. Lystra: Preaching the gospel, their primary mission, took place,

The mound of Lystra located just north of the Turkish village of Hutun Saray. Photo courtesy of holylandphotos.org.

with accompanying miracles to verify the messengers as sent by God. One of these involved a man crippled from his birth. The man leaped and walked upright (straight, erect—*orthos*, medical term used by Doctor Luke) when Paul told him to; the townspeople then tried to treat the preachers as gods. Paul taught them about the vanity of idols, in contrast to the living God, who allowed nations to walk in their own ignorant ways but provided plentiful evidence in the world he created. Trouble-makers from the Jews in Antioch and Iconium came and persuaded the Jews of Lystra to stone Paul, but concerned disciples found him alive outside the city. He and Barnabas later left for Derbe. Be sure to read Paul's comments concerning his difficult experiences and the Lord's help during this section of the journey (2 Tim. 3:10-11).

8. Derbe: By preaching the gospel they made many disciples.

9. Lystra, Iconium, and Antioch: Without distinction as to respective cities, Luke simply records that they made the disciples stronger and urged them to persist in the faith, because of the many tribulations facing all who seek to enter the kingdom of God. The result of such teaching on this second visit was the appointment of elders in each church, not in a district, presbytery, or diocese. The Bible uses three terms interchangeably for elders: *presbuteros* (presbyter, elder), *poimēn (*shepherd, pastor) and *episkopos* (bishop, overseer). There will be fuller discussion of these words at 20:28. They also gave them over to the care of God, in whom they trusted.

Heading Home

10. Perga in Pamphylia: Here again they preached the word on this return visit.

11. Attalia: From this seaport they sailed to Antioch.

Syria

12. Antioch: From this place they had been commended to God's grace for their work on this first trip and had then departed. On this return they gathered the congregation to report to them about the work which God had accomplished in cooperation with them. He had opened a door of faith to Gentiles through the preaching done. Here they stayed a long period—long enough, in fact, for trouble to arise in chapter 15.

View from the east looking west at the unexcavated mound of Derbe (Kerti Huyuk). Early July. Photo and caption courtesy of HolylandPhotos.org.

Define These Words as Used in Relation to Paul's Life

1. Prophet: _____

2. Barnabas: _____

3. John Mark: _____

4. Synagogue: _____

5. Proconsul: _____

6. "God-fearers": _____

7. "Word of this salvation": _____

8. "Shook off the dust from their feet against them": _____
   _____

9. Zeus and Hermes (Jupiter and Mercury in some versions): _____

10. Elders: _____

Discussion Questions

1. Discuss the various hardships of Paul in 2 Corinthians 11, trying to match some of them to different times in his life. _____
   _____

2. What teachers/prophets remained in the church at Antioch after Barnabas and Saul left on their first journey?
   _____

3. Of what value would fasting and laying hands on certain workers be in our time? For what other purposes did some lay their hands on others in the New Testament? _____
   _____

4. Can you cite other instances where archaeologists have unearthed artifacts confirming the biblical record?
   _____

5. What does Luke mean when he says that Elymas tried to turn the proconsul away from the faith? What means might he have used? How do people today make the same effort? _____
   _____

6. Was Paul too stern or harsh in his rebuke of the sorcerer? Should teachers of the word speak like Paul today? Did Paul always employ such language? Cite passages for your answer. _____
   _____

7. Locate all passages mentioning John Mark. How does the New Testament view him? _____
   _____

8. What does Acts 13:48 mean in referring to those who were ordained/appointed/disposed to eternal life? Does the New Testament teach that God says which individuals can be saved, without any exercise of human will?

_____

_____

9. What differences do you observe in Paul's preaching to Jews at Antioch and to Gentiles at Lystra? _____

_____

10. Why did the apostle not mention Jesus to the people of Lystra, as far as we know? _____

_____

11. Why does the Bible refer to idols/idolatry as "vain things" or vanity? Find an Old Testament passage where idols are shown to be vain (worthless). _____

_____

12. When, where, and by whom should elders be appointed? _____

_____

13. Using the different translations of the three Greek words for elders, what can you learn about their work? ___

_____

_____

_____

14. What advantages can you cite in reporting one's work as Paul and Barnabas did in Antioch? _____

_____

A SIDE TRIP TO JERUSALEM (Acts 15:1-35)

While Paul and Barnabas were spending time with the church in Antioch after they had completed their journey, a major problem concerning doctrine and practice arose. When men came from Judea insisting on circumcision after the Mosaic custom, Paul and Barnabas dissented and debated much. It was decided that these men would go with the backing of the congregation to Jerusalem, where they could speak with the apostles and elders about this question. On their way they brought great joy to brethren by their reports of the Gentiles during their earlier journey; finally they reached Jerusalem, where they gave a similar report to the church, elders, and apostles. It was at this point that some of the Pharisees rose up to repeat the insistence that Gentiles also submit to circumcision and the keeping of the Law of Moses.

At a meeting of the apostles and elders to consider this matter, Peter, Barnabas and Paul, and James spoke in declaration of God's will, as the Holy Spirit guided them (v. 28). No church council convened, no consensus-building occurred, no vote took place, and no human creed was ever in view. It is easy for moderns to view this occasion in terms of modern practice; but there is no parallel, for what took place in Jerusalem was divine revelation in relation to the question at hand.

Three Apostolic Arguments

After much debate Peter spoke in verses 7 through 11. His focus was what God had done by him in identifying Gentiles as subjects of the gospel by the Spirit's witness in the tongues spoken at Cornelius's house. In fact, stress seems to be laid on their hearing the same gospel, receiving the same Spirit, and enjoying the same cleansing (15:7-9). He was citing an account of approved action initiated by the Lord. This *approved example* was then used as the basis for the *necessary conclusion* stated in verses 10 and 11. It involved Jews and Gentiles alike being saved in the same manner—through the grace of the Lord Jesus exerted in the gospel, not through the Law. This inference or conclusion was forced (made necessary) by the line of argumentation used by Peter. The only proper conclusion possible was that Peter acted properly in teaching and baptizing Cornelius and not requiring his circumcision. The persuasive effect of such reasoning is seen in the multitude's silence in verse 12.

In verse 12 Barnabas and Paul related God's work through them on their recent journey, recorded in chapters 13 and 14. They gave special attention to the signs and wonders done by the Lord among Gentiles. The Lord's work surely constituted an approved example; by it he gave sanction to the preaching done and the Gentiles as fit subjects of gospel obedience. Though this inference was not stated, it is easily seen as necessary from the premises used and relevant to the issue. Circumcision must not be bound on these Gentiles.

The last speaker was James, who based his speech on a *direct statement* from God recorded in Amos 9. His point was that God was redeeming people who were Gentiles (v. 14), just as Amos had said would happen under the restored tabernacle of David (in the reign of Christ). From this direct statement he then concluded that

they not trouble the Gentiles with Mosaic requirements (vv. 19-21).

The Role of Silence

When the letter was written for distribution to the churches, a disavowal was made of the teaching at issue—namely, that Gentiles needed circumcision to be acceptable to God. Without commandment (authority) from the apostles, the Judaizers had done their teaching. Apart from any apostolic instruction, neither those teachers then nor any teacher today has any right to declare God's will on any matter. The apostles' teaching formed the basis of all approved teaching and authorized action in first-century congregations (Acts 2:42; 1 Pet. 4:11). Also seen in this statement of disavowal in verse 24 is the prohibitive nature of silence. In a time of difference over silence's permissive or prohibitive effect, it can here be clearly seen that, in the absence of divine revelation, man is prohibited from initiating his own idea or way. Nadab and Abihu learned that lesson the hard way (Lev. 10). May we resolve to learn how to discern God's will from the apostles and, having learned it, be content to practice it.

The letter sent by the apostles and elders at Jerusalem carefully set forth the need to abide by certain

principles of truth that had been part of God's will before the Law of Moses came into force. These proscribed practices evidently were some that were prominent in Gentile idolatrous religion. At the same time the letter showed that Gentiles were not bound to keep the Law of Moses, which was never given to any except Israel.

Return to Antioch

Upon their return to Antioch from their very important meeting in Jerusalem, there was joy and encouragement resulting from the letter and from the exhortation of Judas and Silas, who had come from Jerusalem to deliver the letter. Silas, Paul, and Barnabas remained in Antioch, but Judas went back to Jerusalem. There was teaching and preaching of the Lord's word in Antioch for some time before Paul suggested their making another preaching trip.

During this time in Antioch, it does seem that Peter came to Antioch and played the hypocrite in relation to the Gentiles, to retain his Jewish brethren's approval (Gal. 2:11ff.). Paul found it necessary to rebuke Peter in the presence of others for his dissimulation, because Barnabas and others were affected by the lack of straightforwardness in this matter.

Define These Words as Used in Relation to Paul's Life

1. Debate: _____

2. Law of Moses: _____

3. Approved example: _____

4. Necessary conclusion: _____

5. Direct statement: _____

6. Dissimulation: _____

Discussion Questions

1. How do we know that what happened at Jerusalem was not a "church council"?_____

_____

2. How did the inspired men establish what God's will on circumcision was? _____

_____

3. How can we know that the same method of learning God's will operates today?_____

_____

4. What statement did the letter include to demonstrate the lack of authority for the teaching that had been done? What connection does it have to divine silence? _____

_____

5. Cite another example than that of Nadab and Abihu teaching the importance of respecting God's silence.

_____

_____

6. Why could the contents of the letter from Jerusalem be described as both positive and negative?_____

_____

_____

7. Discuss the practices forbidden in the letter and explain why they are still forbidden by the Lord. _____

_____

_____

8. How did the apostle Peter fail to be straightforward about the gospel in Antioch? _____

_____

_____

In a very real sense, this second journey formed a link between the past and the future. Its past association was the attempt to disseminate the revelation given in Jerusalem by apostles and prophets and the re-visiting of churches earlier established on the first journey; its future connection was the plan of Paul and Silas to take the gospel into regions not yet evangelized after going again to some areas already affected by the gospel (all the way to Iconium on the early part of the trip). By the end of this trip of some 2,800 miles, the gospel will have been preached all the way across Asia Minor to the Aegean Sea and then into the continent of Europe, as both Macedonia and Achaia heard the message of Jesus Christ. The student should read Luke's inspired account of this second journey from Acts 15:36 to 18:22.

After sharp contention (*paroxysm*) between Paul and Barnabas concerning again taking John Mark (who had earlier departed—*apostatized* is the Greek word for his physical withdrawal from the journey), the brethren in Antioch commended Paul and Silas (shortened form of Silvanus) to God's grace as they began this journey alone; but they would later gain Timothy and Luke as longtime helpers in teaching the gospel. For approximately three years—probably A.D. 50-54— they would travel, as Paul expressed it, "and see how they are doing" (Acts 15:36). It is clear, however, that Paul's vision also was broader than his original statement of purpose would indicate, in that the trip would encompass new territory, where Christ was not named (Rom. 15:20).

Visiting Established Churches

1. Syria and Cilicia: If this journey took them through Tarsus, the distance would have been 80

Paul Travels The World For Christ (2)

to 90 miles from Antioch. Paul and Silas strengthened the churches in these parts. What an important work it is to help disciples in their spiritual growth. Far too often new converts are left to fend for themselves and new churches to wither from neglect.

2. Derbe and Lystra: Located about 125 miles from Tarsus, here they gained the help of Timothy, "a prize catch." To make him more

New Spiritual Ground

3. Phrygia and Galatia: To reach the first of these regions our preachers traveled some 150 miles to teach where the gospel had never gone, according to the inspired record, though it is possible that some disciples who left Jerusalem in Acts 8 went to these areas. Paul was afflicted by sickness on this first visit to Galatia, but the people well received him (Gal. 4:13-14).

> **What an important work it is to help disciples in their spiritual growth. Far too often new converts are left to fend for themselves and new churches to wither from neglect.**

acceptable to Jewish people who would be hearing them on this trip, Paul had Timothy circumcised. Already a disciple well spoken of by brethren in his area, it would appear that Timothy, whom Paul later called his "son in the faith," was converted on the first trip to this section (Acts 14). From a mixed religious background, he soon committed himself to helping Paul and Silas in the work of the Lord. The decrees from Jerusalem were delivered in letters given to the churches, and congregations grew stronger in the faith of the gospel and in numbers.

Some confusion exists about the reference to Galatia. The regions existing in the earlier days of Roman rule underwent some changes, resulting in new political subdivisions sometimes named for the former regions composing the new subdivisions. Such a change happened to Galatia, so that we cannot be sure whether Luke refers to the old or new area. Since the work of Sir William Ramsay, it seems more likely for the reference to be to the Southern area including Lycaonia, Iconium, Lystra, and Derbe, rather than to the Northern Galatian cities. In

Paul's Second Journey
Outbound
Return

MACEDONIA • Philippi
Berea • • Thessalonica

MYSIA BITHYNIA

Assos • Troas
• Assos •

Aegean
Sea
ACHAIA
Corinth • • Athens

Thyatira • ASIA

GALATIA

CAPPADOCIA

Antioch
• Ephesus
• Miletus PISIDIA Iconium
Patmos Colossae • Lystra • Cilician
Perga • • Derbe Gates
LYCIA Attalia CILICIA
Patara • Tarsus
Knossos Rhodes Seleucia • • Antioch

Crete SYRIA

• Salamis
Paphos •
Cyprus

Great Sea
(Mediterranean)
Scale of Miles
0   200

• Tyre
• Ptolemais
• Caesarea
PALESTINE
• Jerusalem

N
W   E
S

© 2007 MANNA
All Rights Reserved. Used with Permission
www.biblemaps.com

such an event, some of the churches visited would have been works existing from his first journey, with the possibility also being that new works were then begun in the region.

Some scholars believe that Phrygia refers to that part of old Phrygia encompassed in new Galatia, adjoining the border between the Roman provinces of Asia and Galatia. The guidance of the Spirit, usually related to the inspired message delivered by Paul, here also

> **The vision of the Macedonian call meant that Paul's efforts would now shift to the continent of Europe as he crossed the Aegean Sea.**

indicated travel instructions. At a time before going through Phrygia and Galatia ("having been forbidden of the Spirit" in ASV), the Holy Spirit had made it clear that this trip should not extend westward through the province of Asia. The journey through Galatia took Paul and Silas another 150 miles or so, depending on the route used.

4. Mysia: In this northwest area of Asia, having been turned away from Asia, they wanted to turn their attention to the area of Bithynia just over 100 miles to the north, but the Spirit again vetoed Paul's plans. Later developments during the European segment of this trip might shed light upon the Lord's reason for placing Asia off limits for Paul and Silas. Luke records no teaching taking place here.

5. Troas: Situated about 90 miles to the northwest near the coast, Troas formed a watershed

location in terms of a change of venue for this journey. The vision of the Macedonian call meant that Paul's efforts would now shift to the continent of Europe as he crossed the Aegean Sea. Spiritual help was the kind that Paul and Silas were taking everywhere they went, and now they and Luke (first alluded to by "we" at this point) were going to take it to Macedonia, a region north of Achaia (Greece). In this vision the Lord gave clear direction at a time when these men might have grown confused by recent prohibitions. The work done here by Paul and the others is not disclosed; but it would seem that teaching here produced disciples, because of Paul's later visit to an established congregation on the first day of the week in this town.

6. Samothrace ("Thracian Samos," according to Pfeiffer, 221): This was an island situated about 75-80 miles from Troas and about

60 miles from the coast of Thrace in the Aegean Sea. Here Paul and company spent a night on their trip to Europe. Favorable sailing conditions evidently made their travel faster (a two-day trip) than on their return trip in Acts 20:6 (a five-day trip). I conclude that God's providence was "clearing the way" on this journey, knowing that in Philippi waiting there were people who would become Christians and subsequently take the gospel to the very area where Paul was earlier forbidden to go.

7. Neapolis and Philippi: The first, located some 90-100 miles further to the northwest, was the port city for Philippi and is the modern Kavalla. Their sea journey ended here and their land travel resumed inland for ten miles toward their divine destination to which they were called. Philippi, conquered by Philip of Macedon, father of Alexander the Great, in the fourth century B.C. and named for him, came under Roman control two centuries later (Pfeiffer, 221). This valuable outpost (colony) of Rome continued to have Roman privileges and prerogatives in Paul's time. Significant events lay ahead for the apostle to the Gentiles and for the people of the city.

The Conversion of Lydia: Finding women by the river on the Sabbath gave opportunity to teach these Jews of Jesus. No synagogue existed here because of the lack of ten Jewish males, but Paul located the women in their customary place. A business woman named Lydia willingly heard the gospel, which became the means of opening her heart by the Lord, so that she and others in her household then gave attention to what they had learned about following Jesus. Their obedience included baptism into Christ. All actions of the people composing

The Gangitis River near Philippi is where Lydia and her household met for worship on the Sabbath and is most likely where she was baptized.

her household indicate mature people, not infants; this example is no proof of infant salvation or baptism. Lydia's commitment to the Lord then manifests itself in her offer of lodging to her teacher and others in Paul's group and her earnest appeal that they accept it.

The Imprisonment of Paul and Silas: On their way to the place of prayer after Lydia's conversion, Paul and his companions met a slave girl who was possessed by a demon spirit, who thereafter daily acclaimed them to be servants of God proclaiming the way of salvation, as if they were in league with the demon spirit. Annoyed by the persistent problem, Paul cast the spirit out. Trouble arose when the masters of the slave girl, who had been their channel of much profit through her fortunetelling, dragged Paul and Silas into the marketplace and eventually to the magistrates with appropriate false charges, which concealed their true motive. The inflammatory nature of the charges is seen in the result achieved—illegal beating of the men, who were Roman citizens, with rods by lictors after being stripped of their clothing, all

without the benefit of trial. This occasion was one of three times when Paul suffered beating with rods before writing the second letter to Corinth (2 Cor. 11:25). The magistrates (*praetors*) then committed them to the care of the jailer, who placed them in the inner prison (a dungeon, possibly underground) and fastened their feet with stocks. The jailer made sure they could not escape, he thought; but he was not considering the almighty power of the God of Paul and Silas. It is significant that Paul's persecutors in Philippi and in Ephesus later were not Jewish, whereas they were on all other occasions.

The Conversion of the Philippian Jailer: When Paul and Silas were praying and singing hymns to God at midnight, an earthquake, possibly miraculously caused by God, broke up the worship by shaking the foundations of the prison, opening all the doors, and loosing the prisoners' chains. Supposing that his prisoners had all escaped and his own life would be required by the authorities, the jailer started to take his own life, but Paul assured him with loud voice they were all present. The jailer then

This is a portion of the Egnatian Way as it passes through Philippi.

came begging to know what to do to be saved from his sins, not from certain death for allowing prisoners to escape (as some have asserted). He knew of their preaching a message of salvation and knew he needed such salvation, having been awakened by his near death. God's preachers started at point "A" by telling him, "Believe on the Lord Jesus Christ. . . ." In the next verse we learn that they taught him and the rest in his house the word

of the Lord so they might believe, for faith comes from hearing God's word (Rom. 10:17). This obviously penitent jailer then tended to the stripes that the lictors had inflicted, was baptized with his household, and then fed them at his own house. He was a joyous disciple of Jesus Christ. A significant point appears in the final verse of the account of his conversion, as Luke informs us that in doing what he had done, he had believed in God (Acts 16:34).

It is impressive to observe the following: (1) Paul instructed him to believe on Christ (v. 31); (2) He penitently obeyed the Lord in baptism (v. 33); (3) Luke describes his actions as "believing in God" (v. 34). Notice that this individual turned of his own free will, as a result of his decision to hear the word of God. This is the same course followed in the conversion of all candidates for salvation in the Book of Acts.

The Open Departure of God's Men: When the magistrates responsible for the treatment of Paul and

Silas sent for them to be released, the jailer informed them they could leave in peace but Paul refused on the ground that the officials had publicly beaten Roman citizens unconvicted by trial and were now calling for their secret release. He insisted on their honorable handling of this matter by coming and openly releasing the Lord's prisoners. The magistrates complied, asking the men to leave the city. Paul and Silas, without Luke, left by way of Lydia's house, where they saw and encouraged the brethren. What a scene it must have been for these released prisoners, who you would expect to need encouragement, to be imparting encouragement to the recent converts.

8. Amphipolis and Apollonia: These two towns seem to have been points along their journey, though there could have been some teaching here. Each was approximately 30 miles from the previous stop, making the trip to Apollonia some 60 miles in length along the Egnatian Way, an important commercial and military road crossing Macedonia from the Aegean Sea to the Adriatic Sea. Such a distance probably indicated their stopping for the night at one or both of these places. When Paul wrote to the Thessalonians he spoke of the word spreading from that church to Macedonia and Achaia, possibly explaining why, in the divine economy, Paul and Silas did not stop at the two places.

9. Thessalonica: By traveling west for forty miles along the same road, Paul, Silas, and Timothy arrived in Thessalonica (called both Saloniki and Thessaloniki in modern times), Macedonia's most important seaport.

There they followed their custom in going to the Jewish synagogue to reason with the people

Paul traveled over the Egnatian Way, which crossed from the Aegean to the Adriatic Seas, on his way to Thessalonica.

Great Bible Characters: Paul

from the Old Testament writings to explain and prove to them that the Messiah had to suffer and arise from the dead, because they stumbled over the idea of a crucified Messiah (1 Cor. 1:23). His purpose also was to prove that Jesus whom he preached was the very Messiah of the Old Testament prophets. During his three weeks of time doing this work, it seems that a good number of the Thessalonians, including some Jews, many of the devout Greeks (God-fearers as discussed earlier, attracted to the true God), and some of the influential women of the city joined Paul and Silas in their adherence to Christ.

Additional time was then probably used in the ensuing events chronicled by Luke; in fact, Paul's indication was that he stayed in Thessalonica long enough to receive repeated support from the Philippians (Phil. 4:16). There was considerable opposition mustered by the unbelieving Jews who envied the following which Paul gained for Christ. They used some evil men, who probably were loitering in the marketplace, to stir up a mob, set the city in an uproar, and attack the house of Jason to get Paul and Silas, who evidently had lodged there earlier. Their intent was to bring the men out to the people *(dēmos),* which often meant the populace gathered in public assembly to transact public business. When the Jews failed to find their prey, they then dragged Jason and some brethren to the city rulers charging God's preachers with extending trouble from other places to Thessalonica; the accusers were the ones really guilty of stirring up trouble by their trying to whip up the mob. It is interesting that Luke here employs the word *politarchs* for city rulers, though modernistic critics long assailed his

View looking northwest at the excavations of the Forum/Agora. The arched structures are part of the lower (underground) portion of the form. The columns are located on the upper (open air) portion of the forum. A similar style forum has been found at Smyrna. Photo and caption courtesy of HolylandPhotos.org.

inaccuracy in doing so. Seventeen inscriptions using this very term have been discovered in the exact city of whose rulers Luke uses the term (Free 321). The Jews further charged Jason and others with seditious behavior by their claiming Jesus was a king in addition to Caesar. Troubled by this situation, the rulers required some form of security—possibly bail—from Jason to assure either no more trouble, no political subversion of authority, or appearance for later trial (Stringer, 351). Brethren helped with Paul and Silas' departure at night, the situation no longer allowing progress in the gospel.

To this church Paul would later write his first epistle, incorporating the following information, reflecting on his visit:

1. Their receiving the word in much affliction (1 Thess. 1:6).

2. Their turning to God from idols (1 Thess. 1:9).

3. His boldness in Thessalonica

after his treatment in Philippi (1 Thess. 2:2).

4. His support of himself by his own hands (1 Thess. 2:9; 2 Thess. 3:7-9).

5. Their sincere reception of the gospel and suffering for it (1 Thess. 2:13-14).

6. Persecution of Paul and hindrance of the gospel to Gentiles by Jews (1 Thess. 2:15-16).

10. Berea: In the synagogue here Paul found people who were more noble-minded than the Jews in Thessalonica, because they were willing to listen to the message and examine the Scriptures to ascertain its veracity. With such a refreshing view of the Scriptures, many of the Jews turned to Christ, as well as many leading men and women from among the Greeks. All seemed to be fine until the troublemakers from Thessalonica came and caused more trouble here. It does appear that they were acting out their own complaint against Paul and Silas

(17:6). The Christians here then sent Paul away to the sea for his journey, though Silas and Timothy remained here.

11. Athens: Some of the Bereans accompanied Paul on his three hundred-mile trip to Athens and then returned home with Paul's request that Silas and Timothy come to Athens. There is ample evidence that they did join him, though Acts does not mention this matter (I Thess. 3:1-3; Acts 18:5). In the region which the Romans called Achaia (now known as Greece), Corinth was the capital but Athens was the cultural center. To this center of "learning" came men untrained in the philosophy of the Stoics (followers of Zeno), Epicureans (followers of Epicurus), or Plato with a message about the God of the universe and their need for him.

The acropolis at Athens has the famed Parthenon, a temple to Athena, crowning its peak.

business and philosophy were the order of the day.

What Paul saw in this center of human learning and heathen wickedness stirred in him an indignation that called for expression in his message of the true God and the Son of God who came to be the world's Savior. Would it not be helpful if more Christians were moved to

> **Would it not be helpful if more Christians were moved to righteous anger by the religious and moral evil around them to say something to help those caught in the grip of sin?**

While awaiting his companions' arrival, Paul was able to observe some religious traditions of the locals. Along the road entering the city from the sea and in the city proper there were 30,000 different altars dedicated to their various deities, including one "To the Unknown God." Athens was situated around the Acropolis, a hill five hundred feet high with many pagan temples, some of them five hundred years old by then and the Parthenon being the most beautiful (Humble, 128). To the north of that hill was the marketplace (*agora*), where

righteous anger by the religious and moral evil around them to say something to help those caught in the grip of sin? The presence of polytheism (worship of many gods) did not inhibit Paul or squelch the good news of salvation in Christ.

Both the synagogue and the marketplace were the sites where he reasoned with Athenians, who found his teaching of Jesus and the resurrection radically different from their ideas. In something of a backhanded compliment, they called Paul a babbler ("seed-picker"), meaning that they looked on him

as one who had gathered bits and pieces of information here and there but lacking a cogent philosophical framework that could match their own. They brought him to the Areopagus, a civil court that convened to hear and judge on matters affecting the welfare of the city, meeting on the Aeropagus (Hill of Mars). In his situation there is no reason to think they heard charges against Paul, but his "new doctrine." People so enthralled by the world of ideas that they would constantly inquire about what is new, according to Demosthenes, relished such an opportunity. It is highly informative and encouraging to notice what Paul had to say:

A. Their devotion to religion.

B. Information about One they had missed out on.

C. Immense nature and dominion of God.

D. His abundant provision for man, not needing anything.

E. God's making and superintendence of all nations.

F. Man's need to find God, who is near to man as his source.

G. The spiritual nature of God.

H. Time for repentance among those allowed to walk in ignorance of God.

I. Motivation to repent offered in coming judgment, assured by Jesus' resurrection.

His mention of the resurrection piqued their interest, so that they requested another opportunity to hear him. Some became believers, including a member of the court named Dionysius.

12. Corinth: To continue to Corinth, Paul went west about 45 miles to this capital city of Achaia and Roman colony since the rule of Julius Caesar (46 B.C.). What culture was to Athens, vice and corruption were to Corinth, even to the extent that "to live like a Corinthian" became synonymous with participation in the moral corruption and lust so typical of this commercial city. The Temple of Aphrodite (Venus to the Romans) was manned by 1,000 sacred prostitutes encouraging their customers to fulfill their lusts as an act of homage to the goddess, according to the ancient geographer Strabo in his *Geography* (Humble, 143). Paul began his work here "in weakness, in fear, and in much trembling," but he determined to "know nothing except Jesus Christ and him crucified" (1 Cor. 2:3-4).

Paul stood before Gallio's judgment seat at Corinth while at Corinth.

Paul was befriended by Aquila and Priscilla, a couple expelled from Rome by Claudius with all other Jews in 49 B.C. Because the Romans considered Christians to be a sect of the Jews, they viewed religious difference between the Jews and the Christians as disagreements among the Jews. Being of the same craft, that of making tents, Paul lodged with this couple and worked with his own hands to supply his needs, while receiving support from other congregations (2 Cor. 11:8-9). When he wrote the church in Corinth later, he defended his right to receive support for his preaching work (1 Cor. 9:1-15).

His relationship to this husband and wife was an enduring one.

Paul went to the synagogue every Sabbath, so he might reason with the Jews and Greeks there. Teaching God's word for at least a year and a half had a profound effect. His efforts were not appreciated by some who spoke against God's

word; he then turned to Gentiles in Corinth as a whiter field. Among his converts were Justus and Crispus. Justus lived next to the synagogue, and, as a Gentile proselyte who worshiped God there, he was "next to" the Jews. Crispus, whose position was highest in the synagogue, was a "big fish" whom Paul netted. Many Corinthians who heard the word believed and were baptized. Observe this pattern of hearing, believing, and obeying throughout Paul's travels, as well as in the Great Commission and the Epistles of the New Testament.

After sending Timothy to encourage and establish the Thessalonians in their faith, Silas and Timothy returned to Paul from Macedonia, possibly bringing him the support from churches in Macedonia (2 Cor. 11:8-9).

The Lord comforted and encouraged Paul in a vision, after his trying experience with Jewish opponents in Corinth. Christ told him that he would stand by him and help him in teaching the many people who would turn to Christ in this city.

During Gallio's proconsulship (A.D. 51-52, as established by inscription at Delphi telling when he began serving as governor), local Jews mounted more opposition to

Paul set sail for Ephesus from the port at Cenchrea. Phoebe was a member of the church there (Rom. 16:1).

Paul's teaching and brought him before the seat of judgment (*bēma*), which is still standing in the marketplace (Pfeiffer, 173; Humble, 133-134; Jenkins, 17). Here Gallio refused their charge that Paul had taught them to observe practices contrary to Jewish or Roman law (which is unclear), looking at the dispute as involving their own Jewish law. In this matter Gallio behaved himself better than he did in the case of Sosthenes (name appears in an inscription at Corinth, Humble, 144), successor to Crispus, whom the Greeks (or Jews, cf. ASV) beat. In this latter instance the proconsul acted the politician and neglected to stop what the Jews were doing.

After staying here longer, Paul started his trip back to Syria with Priscilla and Aquila accompanying him. By the time he left Corinth, Paul had written both letters to the church in Thessalonica.

Return Trip to Antioch

13. Cenchrea: Before leaving this seaport town, located ten miles from Corinth, Paul shaved his head in support of a vow that he had made. We do not have enough information concerning this vow—its duration, purpose, or setting—to say much about it. There are reasons both for and against its being a Nazirite vow; these the student can explore for himself from Old Testament teaching. Whatever kind of vow it was, we can be assured by the letter from Jerusalem being delivered on this journey that Paul's keeping of it was merely a matter of national custom, not observance of the Law of Moses as a matter of salvation (1 Cor. 9:19-23). It is more beneficial to consider the good work of Phoebe, a servant of the church here (Rom. 16:1-2). It is strange that we sometimes neglect those matters that are revealed while delving into those that are unrevealed.

14. Ephesus: Two hundred fifty miles east across the Aegean Sea was Ephesus, the capital of the province of Asia. Vile and wicked were the ways of this town, partly because of the presence and influence of the Temple of Diana and the statue of Diana (Artemis the Greek name). More along this line will be included later on the third journey. Paul's short stay included some time to instruct the Jews at the synagogue, who, evidently inclined to listen to him more, asked him to stay longer. His haste to reach Jerusalem for some unidentified Jewish feast no doubt found its objective in opportunities to teach his kinsmen the gospel of Christ. Lord willing, he promised to return to spend more time in Ephesus. Paul did leave Priscilla and Aquila here for the good they could do in teaching others.

15. Caesarea: This involved a month's sailing trip of some 600 miles across the Aegean and the Mediterranean to this seat of Roman government, as we later learn from Paul's presence here.

16. Jerusalem: Evidently (see v. 21; "up" and "down") he went the sixty miles southeast up into the mountains of Judea to Jerusalem to greet brethren on this fourth trip here since his conversion.

17. Antioch: He finally ended his trip where he had begun it by traveling approximately 300 miles down to Antioch in Syria. Though no mention of his reporting to the church appears in Luke's record, he might well have done so as on his first trip.

Define These Words as Used in Relation to Paul's Life

1. Silas: _____

2. A.D. 50-54: _____

3. Timothy: _____

4. Southern Galatian cities: _____

5. Macedonian call: _____

6. Aegean Sea, Asia Minor, Europe (map location): _____

7. Conversion: _____

8. Believing in God (Acts 16:34): _____

9. Devout Greeks: _____

10. Politarchs: _____

11. Noble-minded: _____

12. Achaia: _____

13. Babbler: _____

14. To live like a Corinthian: _____

15. Judgment seat: _____

16. Gallio: _____

17. Crispus: _____

18. Sosthenes: _____

19. Vow: _____

20. Diana: _____

Discussion Questions

1. Why were letters being delivered on this second journey? _____

   _____

2. How does Paul manifest his care for the churches on this trip? _____

   _____

3. What lessons can we learn from Paul's comments about John Mark in his writings? _____

   _____

   _____

4. Find the "we" sections of this trip as evidence of Luke's presence. _____

5. When must Timothy have been converted to Christ? What regard does Paul show for him in his various epistles? _____

   _____

6. What reasons can you think of for the Spirit's forbidding Paul and Silas' going to preach in Asia and Bithynia? _____

   _____

   _____

7. Does the Lord still employ visions like the one in Troas to reveal his will? How do you know? _____

   _____

   _____

8. Contrast Paul and Silas' praying and singing in jail with our complaining under similar circumstances. _____

   _____

9. How did the Lord open Lydia's heart? _____

   _____

10. What did (a) Paul do so that the jailer might believe on Jesus Christ and (b) what did the jailer do that was classed by Luke as "believing on the Lord"? _____

    _____

11. Contrast in detail the different receptions given to the word in Thessalonica and in Berea. _____

    _____

12. How is Paul's visit to Thessalonica reflected in his letter to the church?_____

_____

13. Describe the environment in which Paul preached in Athens. _____

_____

14. Summarize his message to the Athenians. _____

_____

15. Why did Paul need divine consolation in the vision from God, both before and after the Lord spoke to him?

_____

_____

16. What advantage is there in training Christians like Aquila and Priscilla to do the Lord's work? _____

_____

17. Explain Paul's strong desire to be in Jerusalem at the time of a feast._____

_____

On his third preaching trip Paul traveled from Antioch through Asia Minor and then to Corinth again, before his return trip to Jerusalem. He spent more time in one city, Ephesus, on this trip than he had spent in any other location on his journeys. Most of this trip was consumed with visits to established congregations, and during this trip Paul spent more time in writing letters than he had on previous trips. The geographical extent of the trip and the length of stay in different locations force us to conclude that he was probably gone close to four years, or from A.D. 54 to 58. Though Acts of the Apostles does not provide us this information, Paul's letters written during this time indicate that he was gathering funds from congregations for distribution to the poor among the saints in Jerusalem. It is also noteworthy that this third journey ended abruptly in Jerusalem with Paul's

Lesson 9

Paul Travels The World For Christ (3)

arrest, making it impossible for him to go on to Antioch in Syria as he had done at the end of his previous journeys. Even then he had opportunities to preach Christ to people of both high and low stations in Jerusalem and other cities where his legal problems would take him, because of his commitment to the Lord's work. The student is urged again to read the biblical account of this trip from Acts 18:23 to 21:29.

The Outbound Trip

1. Antioch of Syria: Paul must have formed a lasting and close relationship to the people in this congregation, for he was with them on several occasions and enjoyed their endorsement and support on his three journeys. I have wondered whether they might have tried to micro-manage his trips, as brethren are sometimes prone to do, or left such matters to the Holy Spirit

Paul Travels The World For Christ (3)

The ancient library of Celsus in Ephesus. A synagogue was located near this library.

complishment during Paul's two to three years in Ephesus was his writing of 1 Corinthians in the spring of A.D. 57 (1 Cor. 16:8), probably waiting for favorable sailing conditions. Other notable occurrences here follow:

Paul directed twelve disciples of John the Baptist to a full relationship to Jesus Christ. These needed to learn that Christ Jesus had now come so they might believe on him, being baptized in his name. After their baptism in the name of Christ, by apostolic hands they received the miraculous powers to speak in other languages and to prophesy. Like Apollos in Acts 18, they were "behind the times" on God's plan to bring the Messiah to be the world's Savior. John had pointed people forward to his death and kingdom, while the apostles began on Pentecost to point people back to the accomplished fact. These twelve of Ephesus had somehow missed out on the Spirit's coming in Acts 2. In the final section of chapter 18, Luke informs us of another resident of Ephesus who ably labored under the same false impression as these twelve disciples. He also received corrective instruction so that he effectively refuted the Jews of Corinth concerning Jesus' identity from the Old Testament writings.

Paul used three months in the synagogue in bold reasoning and persuading concerning the kingdom of God. Some hardened ones refused to believe the message, even speaking evil of the Way of Christ; but others continued learning of him.

For two more years Paul taught daily in the school (lecture hall) of Tyrannus, after strong opposition in the synagogue. He took the disciples with him to the new location. During this time enough people turned to the Lord that Jews and Greeks over the Asian province

and Paul. After some time here, he departed for his home region of Cilicia, through which he had to pass on his way to the regions mentioned in Luke's account. His visit to Antioch this time might have been his final one to the city, as no other visit is recorded. Though we know of others who accompanied Paul on various phases of this trip, no mention is made of Barnabas or Silas in that number.

2. Tarsus: His hometown is nowhere mentioned; but it is unlikely that the trip through its environs did not also include the city of his birth, because he had been there on earlier trips and needed somewhere to spend a night or so. We include it here primarily for measuring distance, approximately 80 to 90 miles.

3. Galatia and Phrygia: Travel through Galatia would likely have taken him to re-visit churches in Derbe, Lystra, Iconium, and Pisid-

ian Antioch, where he strengthened disciples in the faith of Jesus Christ. Such time is not wasted time, nor is time spent in writing letters to churches passed in vain. We must remember that time is needed in these endeavors to remind, warn, encourage, and instruct people. The New Testament places considerable emphasis upon reminding Christians of what they already know. Phrygia, located on the western side of the border of Galatia, close to Pisidia, would have extended his trip farther to the West into Asia Minor.

4. Ephesus: Paul's travel from Tarsus had extended over some 550 miles, depending on his exact route. Luke does inform us that he went "through the upper regions." His return to Ephesus accorded with his promise in Acts 18:21, when he had to leave for the feast in Jerusalem. His time here was spent in teaching the gospel and working with his own hands (Acts 20:34-35). One ac-

heard the gospel of Christ. Converts to Jesus were highly motivated to sound abroad his good news, so that they helped to extend Christ's influence without Paul's travel to some regions.

Paul performed special miracles, causing some to oppose him and others to magnify the Lord Jesus. The miracles were extraordinary in that they depended not on Paul's presence of body, but on articles of clothing that had touched his body, thus linking the miracle with the absent apostle. Seeking to bask in the shadow of Paul's success, some strolling Jews presumed the right to pass themselves off as having genuine powers like Paul's, but their efforts were fraudulent. Demons refused to acknowledge their authority because it was not of Christ or through Paul. Their failure against Paul's success enlarged the Lord's name. When believers saw these notable successes and failures, they proved their repentance by confessing and telling their deeds, with some of them also burning their books of magical spells, rites, and formulas. In this way the word of God powerfully grew and prevailed.

Paul's travel plans are described, after the determination of such (either by the Holy Spirit or his own spirit). He planned to head to Jerusalem after visits to Macedonia and Achaia, and then eventually to Rome. In consideration of his planned trip to Macedonia, he sent Timothy and Erastus there, remaining himself in Asia (Ephesus) for some time. Is it possible that Timothy's travel to Corinth, mentioned by Paul in 1 Corinthians 4:17 and 16:10, took place after his visit to Macedonia with Erastus? Such seems probable from the apostle's instructions about their reception of Paul's young brother. It also appears

The theater in Ephesus would seat 24,000 people. This is the place where Demetrius stirred up the mob to shout "Great is Diana of the Ephesians." The Arcadia Street leads from the theater to the coast. Photo courtesy of HolylandPhotos.org.

from 2 Corinthians 7:13-16 and 8:6 that Paul dispatched Titus and an unnamed brother to the Corinthians after sending them the first letter, to determine their reception of his letter and to urge them to complete their gift for the poor Christians, which Paul was collecting as he traveled.

Paul's preaching brought about strong resistance from the silver-

Diana was also known as Artemis. As is obvious from the picture, Diana was a fertility goddess. Photo courtesy of Mike Hardin.

smiths who even caused a riot in town. Motivated by the covetous spirit, Demetrius aroused workers in his craft to resist Paul's gospel labors, which had already turned many from idols to the living God, thus endangering their livelihood and the renown of Artemis (Diana). Confusion filled the city, followed by a rushing of many into the theater and seizing of Paul's companions. In the midst of their riot, they hailed from the multitude Alexander, a Jew, who tried to make his defense but couldn't for the confusion. The town clerk then urged them to calm down and settle their problems in a lawful assembly (*ekklēsia*), for they were not dealing with violent opponents.

5. Troas: Hopeful of visiting with Titus and learning news of the Corinthians, Paul went north about 200 miles to Troas. He had an open door to preach, but departed for Macedonia when Titus did not arrive (2 Cor. 2:12-13). Here again we depend on a source besides Luke's account to reconstruct Paul's travels and concerns.

6. Macedonia: Some 180 miles distant from Troas lay this European area where he had earlier gone on his second journey. Here again Paul retraced his previous journey to the northwest, probably including visits to Philippi, Thessalonica, and Berea. During this section of his trip, he found great comfort in Titus' report about the Corinthians (2 Cor. 7:2-7), collected funds from the generous Macedonian churches (2 Cor. 8:1-7), encouraged the brethren much, and wrote the Second Epistle to the Corinthians.

7. Illyricum: We include this land mentioned by Paul in Romans 15:19 because of its proximity to Macedonia (about 150 miles to the northwest of Berea), not knowing definitely when Paul preached here. The country which today is called Yugoslavia was known as Dalmatia after the time of Paul's travels.

8. Greece: In Paul's first letter to Corinth, he had promised to return to Corinth, some 400 miles to the south from either Illyricum or Philippi, after passing through Macedonia (1 Cor. 16:5-6). Achaia was the familiar name of this country. Paul's plan to spend the winter

here, coupled with Luke's mention of three months spent here, might indicate that Paul did not include visits to other Christians during this time. Although the letter provides virtually no evidence concerning its time or place of writing, it is possible that the Epistle to the Galatians had its origin during Paul's time here, after he heard of the defection of those people from the gospel (Gal. 1:6). He did write the Letter to the Romans from Corinth, explaining his intent to visit Rome later but now to return to Jerusalem with the funds gathered to serve the poor saints (Rom. 15:25-27). Teaching brought Jewish opposition in the form of a plot against the apostle, probably to be executed either on the way to his ship in Cenchrea or on the ship, because he altered his plans to return to Syria from here, instead going back through Macedonia.

Returning to Syria

9. Macedonia (Philippi): Returning by land was Paul's purpose for the sake of safety. From Greece to Macedonia in the north, he had to travel some 400 miles. With him were six brothers from various congregations, evidently traveling

with him in the collection of funds to provide things honorable in the sight of all (1 Cor. 16:3-4; 2 Cor. 8:18-23). Information concerning some of them is available in Paul's epistles. They left Paul and went ahead of him to Troas. Somewhere in this vicinity Luke rejoins Paul for the rest of his travels in Acts, as seen in his use of "us" and "we." After the Feast of Passover and the seven days' observance connected with it had passed, Paul and Luke departed for Troas.

10. Troas: Paul has now covered the 180 miles between Troas and Philippi enough to be acquainted with the voyage across the Aegean Sea, but this trip required more time than one of his earlier trips (16:11). Here he and Luke stayed seven days, obviously hoping to meet with the saints on the first day of the week to eat the Lord's supper. Here he also had opportunity to teach the brethren and to raise sleeping Eutychus from the dead. When he had eaten a meal before the trip, he then left. Paul's teaching corresponded to his practice in this matter of meeting with Christians on the first day of the week to break bread (1 Cor. 16:1-2; 11:17-34; Acts 20:7). Following this lesson is this author's article "The Significance of the First Day," which the student is urged to study. When all is said and done, the Lord's supper belongs to the Lord's Day. In fact, the possessive "Lord's" is used only twice in the New Testament—of the first day of the week as being the Lord's and of the supper being his also (1 Cor. 11:20; Rev. 1:10).

11. Assos, Mitylene, Chios, Samos, Trogyllium: These towns provided stops, some at night, for the apostle's company as they made their way over some 250 miles by land and by sea to Miletus. At Assos Paul joined them after walking

View of the fishing boats at the port of Dalyan which is the "modern" residential area built upon a portion of Alexandria Troas. Photo and caption courtesy of HolylandPhotos.org.

about twenty miles from Troas. After another thirty miles they arrived at Mitylene, main city on the island of Lesbos, where they anchored for the night. The next day they made it about eighty miles to some place opposite Chios, and the following day probably fifty to sixty miles to the island of Samos. That night they stayed at Trogyllium, located about forty miles to the southeast on land jutting out into the sea south of Ephesus. Close study of this series of stops indicates the reason for some stops at night—the difficulty of sailing between the islands and the mainland on certain segments of the journey.

12. Miletus: Located on the sea some ten to fifteen miles east of Trogyllium and about thirty-five miles south of Ephesus, Miletus became the meeting place of Paul and the elders of the church in Ephesus. It should be easy to discern that the elders knew who they were, thus refuting the idea held by some that elders were just older men in a congregation. If that idea had been held by the church in Ephesus, then who would have known to answer Paul's call? All men in the church except the very youngest ones would have qualified as "elders" in this sense, because all of them were older than someone else. Paul's speech to the elders is remarkable for its content.

A. He reminded them of his manner and method of service to Christ in Ephesus.

B. He had withheld nothing profitable to them of God's entire counsel, thus being innocent of their blood.

C. He clarified his determination to go to Jerusalem in spite of the trouble awaiting him, having been told by the Holy Spirit of such.

D. He indicated this to be his last visit with them.

E. He charged them to be mindful of themselves and of the sheep over which they had been made shepherds, because of voracious wolves who would devour the sheep. Even from among elders would arise men who would selfishly gain a following by their perverse teaching.

F. He commended them to God and to his gracious word in their efforts to make heaven their eternal inheritance.

> He charged them to be mindful of themselves and of the sheep over which they had been made shepherds, because of voracious wolves who would devour the sheep. Even from among elders would arise men who would selfishly gain a following by their perverse teaching.

G. He reminded them of Jesus' words to motivate their spirit of giving in efforts to hold up the weak ones.

After prayer together and their tearful farewell, they walked with him to the ship.

13. Cos, Rhodes, Patara in Lycia: These towns and islands were mentioned by Luke primarily as part of his detailed record of the route being followed, because he tells us nothing about Paul's work in these parts. From Cos to Rhodes he traveled 65 miles; from Rhodes to Patara, about 100 miles. In Patara he made a change of ships, probably finding a larger one for use on the open sea during his return voyage to Palestine.

14. Tyre in Phoenicia and Syria: Maps of New Testament times show Tyre, once a Phoenician city, situated in Syria. The sea voyage covered some 350 to 400 miles,

passing to the south of Cyprus. This final section of Paul's sea journey required four to five days of favorable sailing weather. Finding disciples here, Paul and the rest stayed for seven days as they had done in Troas, possibly for the same purpose, but definitely having occasion to meet with their brethren to eat the Lord's supper. They also told Paul that he should not go to Jerusalem, having learned from the Spirit that trouble lay ahead (cf. 20:22-23). It is unlikely that the Spirit here forbade Paul's going to Jerusalem, because his customary practice was to heed the Holy Spirit's directions concerning his travels. The disciples here loved Paul for his work, as seen in their taking families on the walk out of town with him and praying with him.

15. Ptolemais: Thirty miles along the coast to the south, Paul and the others stayed with the Christians for a day before moving on toward Jerusalem.

16. Caesarea: By land (over arduous terrain) or by sea (to an excellent seaport) the group moved on some 45 miles for Paul's third visit to Caesarea (Acts 9:30; 18:22). Here they abode many days with Philip the evangelist, who had previously lived in Jerusalem. While here, a poignant event occurred with Agabus' coming from Judea to tell Paul about his being handed over to the Gentiles, the brethren's warning him not to go there, and Paul's ready resignation to die for the name of the Lord Jesus. His brethren finally stopped their protest and prayed for the Lord's will to be done.

17. Jerusalem: Travel here by foot covered about 60-65 miles, gradually ascending to the city, situated 2,400 feet above sea level. William Ramsay thought that Luke's verb ("took up our carriages," Acts 21:15) expressed the packing of a horse for travel, because of its use in this way in classical Greek; but evidence is lacking for such meaning in the common Greek of Luke's time. If animals were used to carry the burden, one would have to learn such from other sources than Luke's verb. The disciples from Caesarea brought Paul to Mnason, a veteran or early disciple, to lodge with him (consider the better rendering than that of the KJV, according to A.T. Robertson's *Word Pictures*, Vincent's *Word Stud-ies in the New Testament*, and W. Robertson Nicoll's *The Expositor's Greek Testament*). Here a series of related events took place.

When Paul reported God's work among the Gentiles by his ministry, those gathered at James' house glorified the Lord. They then suggested to Paul that he take action to demonstrate that he was not trying to influence the Jews to forsake their customs relating to Moses, including circumcision.

Paul agreed to participate with four men in fulfilling a vow; and when he went into the Temple to announce the completion of the purification, Jews from Asia found him and seized him, falsely accusing him of bringing Greeks into the Temple. Paul's arrest by the commander (chief captain) terminated his journey, because his return to Antioch as on the former journeys was now impossible. He began a series of hearings here and elsewhere, leading eventually to his Roman imprisonment.

We must understand Paul's actions as illustrating his clear teaching in passages like 1 Corinthians 9:19-23. His avowed intention was to save more people by becoming their servant, whether of the Jews or the Greeks. Paul did observe the Law of Moses at times on certain points, not as religious practice necessary to salvation but as national custom. He had Timothy circumcised on one hand, but on the other hand he refused to yield on the matter of Titus' circumcision (Acts 16:3; Gal. 2:3-5). On the other hand, one who depended upon the Law for justification, by obligating himself to keep the whole Law perfectly, became estranged from Christ, fell from grace, and profited nothing from Christ (Gal. 5:1-6).

Define These Words as Used in Relation to Paul's Life

1. Antioch in Syria: _____

2. Cilicia: _____

3. Phrygia: _____

4. Apollos and twelve disciples in Ephesus: _____

   _____

5. School of Tyrannus: _____

6. Artemis: _____

7. Macedonia: _____

8. Achaia: _____

9. "We" passages in record of Paul's journeys: _____

   _____

10. Eutychus: _____

Discussion Questions

1. Cite two or three passages from Paul's epistles to show that he was gathering relief funds for poor saints from churches on this third journey. _____

2. Cite two or three instances in which his epistles help us to know of his travels, when Luke said nothing about the specific details. _____

_____

3. Why would Paul have re-visited the Galatian cities where he had planted the seed of the kingdom? _____

_____

_____

4. When Paul taught the gospel in the school of Tyrannus with whatever support he received from congregations, were the churches supporting the school? _____

_____

5. Explain why the special miracles of Paul at Ephesus involved the use of something that had touched him.

_____

_____

6. How did the former practitioners of the magical activities in Ephesus prove their repentance? _____

_____

7. When Paul departed from Macedonia the final time, why and how did he change his plans? _____

_____

_____

8. How does Luke teach us something about the Lord's supper by approved example in Acts 20:7? Is he also teaching us to eat the supper in an upper room? Why the difference?_____

_____

9. Discuss what significance the first day of the week has always had for Christians. _____

_____

10. How did the congregation in Ephesus know who its elders were? _____

_____

11. What do we learn about the work of elders from Paul's address to elders in Acts 20? _____

_____

12. With the different warnings concerning the trouble facing him in Jerusalem, why do you think he persisted in going there? _____

_____

13. Why did Paul agree to the elders' suggestion about the vow?_____

_____

14. What results follow when one attempts to be justified by the Law of Moses, as in circumcision for the sake of salvation? _____

_____

15. Is justification by any law, even the law of Christ, possible? (Remember that justification by works of law—any law—requires flawless works, no sin at all. Consult Galatians 3:10 for the principle of legal justification.)

_____

16. Why can it be said that Paul's trip ended prematurely in Jerusalem in Acts 21?_____

The Significance of the First Day of the Week

The first day of the week has a special place in the economy of the new covenant. It took the place of the special day observed under the first covenant—not in the sense of being like it in all respects, but in its being a day of special observance. Among the factors contributing to the importance of the first day of the week are the following.

The Resurrection of Jesus

Mark 16:9 shows that Jesus arose from the grave on the first day of the week. Luke 24:1, 13, 21, and 46 all together demand our belief that Jesus arose on the first day, not on the Sabbath or on some other day, as some insist. Verse 1 sets the stage by identifying the day as the first day of the week; verse 13 shows that on that first day two disciples walked to the village of Emmaus. In their conversation with Jesus, who was then not disclosed to them, they referred to the first day as the third day since Jesus' crucifixion (v. 21).

In the remarks of Jesus himself in verse 46, we learn that his resurrection was an event of the third day. By Jesus' statement of verse 46 and the disciples' identification of this first day of the week as the third day, we have to conclude then that Jesus arose on the first day of the week, not on the seventh day. The first day derives its significance from that momentous event of the resurrection of Jesus, in keeping with Old Testament prophecy.

The Acknowledging of Jesus

Psalm 2:7 refers to the resurrection of Jesus and to his being thereby begotten that very day, though the rulers had taken counsel against the Father and against his anointed one, the Christ. Acts 13:32, 33 confirms that the second Psalm, particularly the word "begotten," refers to the resurrection of Jesus. In that glorious event God was acknowledging to all men for all time to come that Jesus was his Son with authority (Rom. 1:4). The first day is made even more important by God's acknowledgement concerning Jesus in the event of this day.

The Appearances of Jesus

Jesus' appearances to Mary Magdalene (Mark 16:9) and to another Mary (Matt. 28:9, 10), who worshiped him; to the two disciples on the road to Emmaus (Luke 24:13-15); to the ten apostles (Luke 24:33-36; John 20:19); and to all of the apostles after eight days (John 20:26) in substantiation of his resurrection make the day all the more significant.

The Events of Pentecost

According to Leviticus 23:15, 16, the day of Pentecost came on the first day of the week—that is, seven Sabbaths and one day after the Sabbath connected with Passover.

On the first Pentecost after the resurrection, the Holy Spirit was given in fulfillment of Joel's prophecy (2:28-32; Acts 2:1-4). Christ's rule as high priest and king was announced as beginning (Zech. 6:13; Acts 2:29-36). The new covenant went into effect (Isa. 2:3; Luke 24:47, 49; Acts 2:38). The church (mountain of the Lord's house, Isa. 2:2, 3) was established in the last days (Acts 2:17, 41, 47).

Action of Local Churches

From these four considerations, it should be clear why the first day of the week had a place of special significance in the life of the New Testament church. The church having been established on this day, we are not surprised to learn that local congregations of the Lord's people met on this same day to remember Christ in eating the Lord's supper and to contribute of their financial means to support the Lord's work (Acts 20:7; 1 Cor. 16:1-2). Paul met with the Christians in Troas, thereby giving apostolic sanction to what there transpired.

Does it have that place in your life? People faithful to Christ will meet on the first day of the week as first-century Christians did for the purposes assigned by the apostles of Christ. They will not seek to evade God's will in this matter or to substitute their own way for his way. In doing what the New Testament authorizes there is fellowship with God, but in altering the plan there is no assurance of such.

Paul's Arrest and Trials (1)

time covered by this series of events chronicled by Luke in Acts 21:30 to 28:31 seems to extend from A.D. 58 to A.D. 63 or 64. Students should carefully read the narrative of Luke, as well as Paul's own comments on his sufferings.

In this lesson we examine Paul's visit to Jerusalem and then his trip as a prisoner to Caesarea. In the second lesson under this title, we shall cover his trip to Rome and his stay there for two years.

After Paul's third journey was prematurely terminated by his Temple arrest, there ensued a long and arduous series of trials, which included false accusations against him, a mob's attempt to kill him, speeches and appearances before the people and the Sanhedrin, travel to Caesarea to evade a Jewish plot, accusations by a lawyer/orator, hearings before Governor Felix and Governor Festus, his defense before King Agrippa, a long and treacherous voyage to Rome, shipwreck during the voyage, and his two

years' wait in Rome to have his appeal heard by Caesar. The detailing of these vicissitudes does not mean that Paul did not also enjoy blessings and opportunities during this time; but hardship was dominant in this phase of his life, for he went through it all as a prisoner of Jesus Christ. Such sufferings and labors of the apostle remind us of his writing concerning such matters in 2 Corinthians 11:23-28 and they cause many to wonder why the apostle was not more discouraged than he was (2 Cor. 4:8-12). The

The Visit to Jerusalem

The following analysis of Paul's visit to Jerusalem from the termination of his third journey in A.D. 58 will chronicle his movements until it becomes necessary for him to leave Jerusalem.

The Arrest in Jerusalem: Paul's arrest took place while he was in the Temple in Jerusalem declaring the fulfillment of days of purification connected with a vow. Evidently before the offering was brought for Paul and the four men, Jews from Asia stirred up the people and tried to capitalize on this opportunity to finish the work of murdering Paul which they left incomplete during his lengthy visit to Ephesus in Acts 19 (cf. Acts 20:18-18).

They falsely charged Paul with teaching all against the Jews, the Law, the Temple, and with defiling the Temple with Greeks whom he brought there. The falsity of the first three charges can be seen in Paul's present activity in their Temple, designed to show his love for his people and for their customs, though he would

Jerusalem as seen from the Mount of Olives. The domed building in the center is the Dome of the Rock, a Muslim holy site.

disavow any justification under the Law. Their accusation about the Greeks was based on their wicked supposition that he had brought Trophimus, with whom they had seen him earlier in Jerusalem in the Temple. People operating under such vicious motive and mind then rushed to seize Paul and drag him from the Temple, then attempting to kill him.

When the military commander learned of their efforts, he brought soldiers and centurions sufficient for the job to rescue the apostle. Upon seeing the approaching soldiers, the Jews quit their beating of Paul. The commander inquired of Paul's identity and deeds, only to incite further the mob's response to such a level of confusion that he was unable to learn the truth. Soldiers had to carry Paul to keep him safe from the tumultuous mob demanding his death. On the way into the Tower of Antonia (castle, barracks, fortress), Paul had occasion to correct the false impression of the officer that Paul was an Egyptian terrorist/assassin. After he told him of his race and hometown, he asked permission to speak to the Jewish mob.

Paul's defense on the castle steps: After receiving the silence of his audience, Paul spoke to them in Hebrew concerning his former life as a persecutor among them, his conversion to Jesus Christ, his commission as an apostle, and his early troubles among the Jews in Jerusalem. Important details are here stressed.

He first established his Jewish associations with these Jewish listeners. He did this by telling of his Jewish upbringing in Tarsus, his training by Gamaliel in Jerusalem, and his violent persecution of the Christians to the time of his conver-

This a balustrade from the Jerusalem Temple which was placed to mark the area in which Gentiles were not allowed to enter. The inscription said that whoever passed beyond this balustrade was responsible for his own death. Paul was charged with bringing a Gentile into the Temple. Photo courtesy of HolylandPhotos.org.

sion, in cooperation with Jewish authorities.

Paul then showed them how his turn from the life of a persecutor was not on a whim, but the result of miraculous revelation from God. The Lord even informed Paul that he had been persecuting the Christ. He then gave Saul orders to enter Damascus, where he would have Ananias (devout according to the Law and well-attested by the Jews)

ready to impart further instruction to him and restore his sight. Paul had been God's choice to see the Lord, hear his voice, and serve as a witness to all people. He then called upon the Lord for salvation by arising in his penitence to be baptized.

While praying in a trance (*ekstasis*) after his return to Jerusalem, Paul heard the Lord say to leave Jerusalem quickly because the people there would refuse to hear

When Claudius Lysias arrested Paul, he allowed Paul to speak to the Jews on the steps of the Tower of Antonio, which was on the northwest side of the Temple.

Paul's Arrest and Trials (1)

him. Paul's subsequent hesitancy to leave, based on his previous associations with the Jewish cause, brought no change of mind in the Lord, only repeated instruction to leave for distant places to teach Gentiles. Until this bit of information from Paul the Jewish audience was listening, but they heard something that caused them to "turn him off."

Uproar following and Paul's affirmation of Roman citizenship: The cause of this uproar was Paul's reference to Christ's sending him to take the gospel to the Gentiles. Their polite hearing suddenly became a request for Paul's death, as one not fit to live. They cried out,

Paul had been born a citizen, receiving his citizenship from some ancestor through his own father. Those planning to scourge Paul then left, and even the commander was fearful because of his order to bind Paul. He would make other arrangements to learn of the reason for Paul's accusation by the Jews.

Paul's appearance before the Sanhedrin: On the following day the commander commanded the Sanhedrin to meet to learn why Paul was the object of Jewish opposition. The hearing began with interplay between Paul and the high priest, but then antipathy between the Pharisees and the Sadducees took over.

regard his conscience as important, by his guarding it, regarding it, and keeping it pure (Acts 24:16). Failing to thus treat it renders it useless, for it becomes seared as with a hot iron (1 Tim. 4:2).

Paul then rebuked Ananias for his hypocrisy, only to receive rebuke for his disrespectful remarks to the high priest. For some unexplained reason, Paul had not known who this man was.

In the face of such opposition, Paul knew the impossibility of receiving fairness from this body; he then used the essential differences between the two main groups on the Sanhedrin, Pharisees and Sadducees, to divide them. He affirmed his belief in the resurrection—one which he had long shared with the Pharisees. Such a hope of being raised from the dead, along with the existence of spirits and angels, supported in the Old Testament but clarified and strengthened in the New Testament, was crucial to the preaching done by Paul. Those of the sect of the Pharisees then conceded that an angel or spirit might have spoken to Paul, and that to oppose him in such a case would be to oppose God. Much dissension then arose in the Sanhedrin, causing the commander to order Paul to be brought to the safety of the barracks.

God's revelation to Paul that he would bear witness in Rome: On the night after Paul's appearance before the Jewish Council (Sanhedrin), the Lord saw fit to reveal himself and his plans to the imprisoned apostle.

The time for this divine revelation was undoubtedly one of discouragement. He had been arrested in the Temple, assailed by the mob, assaulted by the soldiers, and apprehended to prevent his assas-

> **Paul's conscientiousness covered the entirety of his life—his life in Judaism and his life as a Christian.**

tore their clothing from their bodies, and cast dust into the air.

The military commander commanded Paul to be brought into the barracks so that he could learn why the mob so intensely opposed Paul. Scourging was the method that he would employ to ascertain information from the prisoner; it would be administered by means of a whip, consisting of leather straps to which were attached pieces of metal or bone. As Paul's body was tied in a tightened position for the scourging, Paul asked the centurion whether it was legal to scourge an uncondemned Roman citizen.

After hearing this first indication of Paul's Roman citizenship, the officer then spoke to the commander, who talked to Paul about this matter. The commander had purchased his citizenship, while

Paul's affirmation of a good conscience in all that he had done was too much for the high priest, who commanded someone to slap Paul on the mouth. Paul's conscientiousness covered the entirety of his life—his life in Judaism and his life as a Christian. Ananias did not appreciate such concern for right or the sting that Paul's statement brought to him. Conscience is a spiritual faculty with which God has endowed all humans, because they are created in his image (Gen. 1:26-27). It serves as a monitor of one's thoughts, words, and actions, either to approve or to disapprove by the application of a standard which one has accepted (Rom. 2:15). In other words, the conscience is from God; but one's training/teaching forms the content/framework of his conscience, explaining why one person accepts one belief while another rejects it. One must

sination—all of this either by the Jews or because of them. When his former friends treated him in this way (people whom he called his "own countrymen" in 2 Cor. 11:26), especially when he was trying to help them, would he not have become discouraged?

The Lord's words should have been quite encouraging to Paul: "Be of good cheer, Paul; for as you have testified for Me in Jerusalem, so you must bear witness also at Rome." While Paul had earlier spoken of his desire to travel to Rome after Jerusalem, he had not then known the conditions under which he would make the trip. Now it might have been dawning on him that he would go as a prisoner. For this time and the future, however, God had an objective in mind and the means of attaining it—all in his providence—for the good of Paul, for the good of his people, and for the good of his cause.

Soon after the Lord was comforting his apostle, discomfort was in the making through a Jewish plot to take his life. More than forty Jews took an oath not to eat or drink until they had murdered him. They attempted to enlist some of the Jewish leaders on the Sanhedrin to appeal to the military commander to ask for Paul to be brought to them for another round of questioning on the next day, so that they could lie in wait to assassinate him as he drew near to the place of meeting.

Paul's nephew discovers a Jewish plot to kill Paul: It was Paul's sister's son (only N.T. reference to Paul's family) who first learned of their conspiracy to ambush his uncle and brought word of it to Paul in the barracks. Paul then asked a centurion to take his nephew to the commander to tell him of the plot. In private he learned

The remains of Herod the Great's palace at Caesarea on the coast are still visible. After Judea was placed under the administration of procurators, they ruled from Caesarea where Paul was taken for safe keeping following his arrest in Jerusalem.

from Paul's nephew of the plot, with his warning not to comply with the request of the murderous Jews. He then required the young man to divulge to no one the information

chain of divine providence was the military arrangement provided for Paul's safe conveyance to Caesarea, where he would have his case heard by Governor Felix.

> While Paul had earlier spoken of his desire to travel to Rome after Jerusalem, he had not then known the conditions under which he would make the trip. Now it might have been dawning on him that he would go as a prisoner.

which he had brought, probably for the young man's safety and for greater efficiency in dealing with the plot. Two links in the chain of divine providence have already manifested themselves for Paul's welfare—the nephew's discovery and the commander's kind consideration of Paul. Such are the means employed by God in ruling and overruling for the good of his people.

Commander sends Paul to Caesarea: Another link in the

Four hundred seventy soldiers went with Paul for the thirty-nine miles of the journey to Antipatris, where there was more likelihood of the conspirators' acting out their plot, with only the cavalry escort accompanying the apostle the remaining twenty-six miles. Animals were also provided for Paul and possibly his guard to ride.

Claudius Lysias, identified as the commander (chief captain) in his letter to Felix, informed the governor (procurator) of the matters relevant to Paul's case. He did so accurately, for the most part; but he misinformed Felix about his motivation in rescuing Paul. He had learned of his Roman citizenship only after the rescue when he ordered Paul to be examined by scourging. He obviously was seeking to place himself in the best light possible.

Prisoner in Caesarea

After Paul's arrival in the seacoast city of Caesarea, events began to point toward Rome. Close study of the inspired text will show the following series of major events

> **Paul reasoned with them concerning righteousness, self-control, and the coming judgment; a terrified Felix passed Paul off and said he would send for him at a convenient time.**

happening during his two years here.

Paul awaiting trial: Upon their arrival in Caesarea, the horsemen delivered Paul and the letter to Governor Felix, who had become governor in A.D. 52. After Felix read the letter, he inquired of Paul's home province and learned that it was Cilicia, which lay within his own jurisdiction. He then waited for the arrival of Paul's accusers, who most likely learned from the commander of Paul's trip there and their need to go there after Paul was at a safe distance from them. Paul was kept prisoner in Herod's Praetorium, so called because Herod the Great had built it much earlier. Five days after Paul's arrival the Jews sent by Claudius Lysias came with an orator named Tertullus to present their evidence against Paul to Felix.

Tertullus' charges against Paul: This hired orator, probably not much trained in the field of law, was there for his speaking expertise. His flattery was probably not lost on the brutal and corrupt governor, who did not deserve such but still relished it. His charges against Paul were threefold: (a) He was a plague, causing problems like a plague or a pestilence does, working against the welfare of the people; (b) He was a creator of dissension (strife, discord) among the Jews all over, not just in Judea; and (c) He was a ringleader of the sect of the Nazarenes (possibly a derisive term used of followers of Jesus, who came from Nazareth, a lowly town). The statement that Paul had tried to profane the Temple was part of the evidence sustaining the charges lodged. Tertullus even incorporated the effort of the Jews to judge Paul by their own law until the commander's rescue of the apostle. Notice carefully his misrepresentation by attributing violence to the commander and honorable dealings to the Jews, while the opposite was really the case. To the language of this rhetorician the Jews added their assent.

Paul's defense before Felix: Paul first addressed the charges against him and then turned to explain his life, work for Christ, and purpose for being in Jerusalem.

Granted an opportunity to speak, Paul proceeded to base his defense on (a) his lack of time to carry out the destructive program which Tertullus had charged him with leading, which also gave opportunity to investigate Paul's activities and (b) their complete lack of evidence to sustain the charges. They had not found Paul disputing or inciting the people in the Temple, the synagogues, or the city.

His personal defense then turned into a defense of the Lord and his cause. Paul reached back to God's Old Testament purpose to show the unity existing between that and its New Testament fulfillment by confessing that he worshiped "the God of my fathers, believing all things which are written in the law and the Prophets." He further affirmed his hope of a resurrection of all dead, even as his enemies believed. Because of that hope, he tried to keep his conscience free from blame in reference to God and man.

Paul finally moved to explain the circumstances surrounding his presence in Jerusalem—his bringing funds to relieve the needs of saints in Jerusalem ("my nation"). While there he did go to the Temple for reasons earlier explained, giving his enemies the opportunity which they sought. He was in the Temple, however, "neither with a multitude nor with a tumult."

He then called upon his opponents to speak of any wrongdoing found in him before the Jewish council, finally identifying the one sore spot between them (the Sadducees part of the Sanhedrin) and him—his belief in the resurrection of the dead.

Felix's deferral of the case: Because he understood more about the way of Christ and his followers than earlier (or than others understood), the governor could see that Paul's guilt had not been established by his enemies and that the difference between them was a matter of religious teaching.

On this basis he claimed that he was postponing his decision in Paul's case until the commander could arrive; but there is no record of his arrival or of a continued hearing. In view of Luke's indicating Felix's motive to be one of greed in later verses, it is highly probable in this writer's judgment that his greed was already showing itself in this earlier instance.

Felix did allow Paul some supervised freedom during this wait, so that friends could visit him to aid him and surely to be encouraged by him.

The apostle also had opportunity to speak to Felix and his (third) wife Drusilla, whom he had urged to leave her husband. They sought him out to learn from him about the faith in Christ. Paul reasoned with them concerning righteousness, self-control, and the coming judgment; a terrified Felix passed Paul off and said he would send for him at a convenient time. At this point we know for sure that the governor is looking for bribe money to gain Paul's release; frequent calls for Paul to teach him resulted. For two years Paul remained in prison in Caesarea, and for some of this time the governor sought a bribe. Porcius Festus, a more prudent ruler, became Felix's replacement in A.D. 58 or 59.

Paul's hearing before Festus: The new governor moved quickly to form a relationship with the Jewish leaders in Jerusalem and consider Paul's case, after their informing him of their side.

They urged him to cooperate with them in bringing Paul to Jerusalem for further hearing, so they could once again seek to kill the apostle. Festus refused, saying

that he intended soon to leave for Caesarea, where Paul was staying. He invited their authorities to come to Caesarea to accuse Paul, to see if he had fault.

Less than eight to ten days later (ASV) Festus went down to Caesarea and the next day asked for Paul to be brought before him. The Jews from Jerusalem made serious allegations about Paul but were again unable to prove them. Paul's response was that he had committed no offense against the Law, the Temple, or Caesar. Unable to grant an earlier favor requested

His life from that time had been one of declaring to all the need to repent, turn to God, and do works suitable for repentance. In his teaching he was "testifying to small and to great" nothing except what the prophets and Moses predicted concerning Christ's suffering, resurrection, and gospel.

by the Jews (25:3), Festus tried to work himself into their favor by asking Paul to go to Jerusalem to be tried before him. Paul, knowing the unlikelihood of a fair hearing in that political climate, refused the governor's request and appealed to Nero Caesar. His stated reason was that Festus knew he had done nothing wrong against the Jews; he did not refuse to die for something worthy of death. In consultation with his council, the governor granted Paul's appeal, which was not based on any sentence issued.

Festus' relating of Paul's case to Agrippa: King Agrippa II was the son of Agrippa I in Acts 12 and the brother of Bernice, with whom rumor said he was living in incest. She had earlier been married to

her uncle, the brother of Agrippa I. Agrippa and Bernice came to pay their respect to the new governor of one small part of King Agrippa's domain and after many days learned of Paul's case from Festus.

Festus might have misrepresented the matter of the judgment asked for by the Jewish leaders (v. 15), and he omitted his motive of pleasing the Jews in the matter of his request that Paul go to Jerusalem for judging (v. 20). He did acknowledge his unfamiliarity with such a matter of the Jews' religion, which was the basic issue involved in the charges against Paul (19- 20).

Agrippa asked for opportunity to hear Paul's case and did so the next day in the presence of several prominent city leaders, both military and governmental. Festus began the proceedings by informing the king that he had learned nothing worthy of death in Paul, in spite of the Jewish demand that he die for his crimes. He was now seeking some explanation upon which he could base charges to send to Nero Caesar (the "Augustus" of verses 21 and 25, though he is here designated such by a term of respect used by many different Caesars; he was not the Augustus of Luke 2:2).

Agrippa's hearing of Paul's case: The apostle felt fortunate to present his case to one so knowledgeable of Jewish customs and questions. In the speech of the apostle before the king one can read one of the truly great orations of history.

First Paul spoke of his early life as a Pharisee in Jerusalem, which all the Jews knew about. He did this to link their hope, based on God's promise to their fathers (beginning with Abram), to his current teaching of the resurrection, the fruition of that promise/hope. In other words, he was simply setting forth the culmination of all that preceded Christ in Old Testament times. In that vein he asked the king why it was so incredible that God should raise the dead.

He then considered his opposition to Christ and Christians, which he truly thought he must do (matter of conscience, as in 23:1 and 24:16). His zeal took him to foreign cities to oppose them, as on his trip to Damascus when the Lord appeared to him.

In detail he described the miracle along the Damascus road and his obedient response to the heavenly vision. His life from that time had been one of declaring to all the need to repent, turn to God, and do works suitable for repentance. In his teaching he was "testifying to small and to great' nothing except what the prophets and Moses predicted concerning Christ's suffering, resurrection, and gospel.

Festus then interrupted with his opinion that Paul was speaking as a maniac, too engrossed in his study of the Law and the Prophets. After all, he had spoken of a vision from heaven and of Jesus arising from the grave. Paul replied that he spoke words of truth (reality) and reason (a sound mind) and confronted the governor with the fact that these events had not occurred in a corner.

Paul next turned to King Agrippa to ask him about his belief of the prophets, even affirming his confidence in the king's belief, before the king spoke of his nearness ("in a little") to becoming a Christian. Paul's fervent wish, both stated and exemplified in his efforts, was that all would become followers of Christ.

The consensus of the entourage was that Paul was innocent of anything worthy of death, and Agrippa thought Paul might have been freed without his appeal to Caesar.

Define These Words as Used in Relation to Paul's Life

1. Sanhedrin: _____

2. Asia: _____

3. Trophimus: _____

4. Tower of Antonia: _____

5. Ananias: _____

6. Trance: _____

7. Paul's nephew: _____

8. Claudius Lysias: _____

9. Antipatris: _____

10. Herod's Praetorium: _____

11. Tertullus: _____

12. "Alms to my nation": _____

13. Porcius Festus: _____

14. Caesar: _____

15. Agrippa and Bernice: _____

16. Augustus: _____

Discussion Questions

1. How long did the series of trials beginning in Acts 21 continue? _____

2. How did Paul view his troubles in his own writings? Name at least five of these troubles. _____

_____

_____

3. Explain the circumstances of Paul's appearance in the Temple. _____

_____

4. Why is it reasonable to think that Paul probably had seen the Jews from Asia before their Jerusalem effort to
   kill him? _____

_____

5. Identify the false charges lodged against Paul and demonstrate them to be false._____

_____

6. Why can it be said that the commander befriended Paul? _____

_____

7. How did Paul try to identify his oneness with his Jewish listeners? _____

_____

8. Explain the Damascus road miracle recounted by Paul and discuss its purpose in his conversion and apostleship. _____

_____

9. Why do you think the Lord persistently told Paul not to remain in Jerusalem at such an early time in his ministry? _____

_____

10. Why did the Jews hearing Paul's speech quit listening to him? Cite instances in which people today act simi-
    larly. _____

_____

11. Is it right for a Christian to depend on his citizenship to escape persecution?_____

_____

12. How did the Jews show their hatred for Paul after his mention of the Gentiles? How do some today react hate-
    fully to teachers of truth? _____

_____

13. How was scourging carried out? How did it produce evidence in the examination?____ _____

_____

14. What kind of military official do you think the commander was? Provide evidence. _____

_____

15. Discuss the meaning, function, basis, and guarding of conscience. _____

_____

_____

16. How did Paul use the composition of the Sanhedrin to his advantage? Why did he claim to be a Pharisee? ___

_____

17. What does the Lord's comforting message to Paul at his time of need tell us about God? _____

_____

18. Identify the links in the chain of God's providence discussed in this lesson. Do you find others? _____

_____

_____

19. What were the three charges that Tertullus made against Paul? _____

_____

20. Why should we try to do as Paul did in maintaining a conscience without offense toward God and men? ____

_____

21. Discuss the wisdom of Paul's using his belief held in common with the Pharisees—resurrection of the dead—as he spoke before Felix. _____

_____

22. What kind of person and ruler was Felix? Is one the result of the other? _____

_____

23. How would you describe the charges twice made against Paul, in view of the lack of evidence for them? ____

_____

24. Why did Festus want Agrippa to hear Paul's case? _____

_____

25. In Paul's defense before Agrippa, what evidences do you notice that Paul thought Agrippa had some faith?

_____

_____

26. Explain how Paul's teaching and hope were what the Law and Prophets had anticipated. _____

_____

_____

Paul's Arrest and Trials (2)

After finishing most of his third journey, we have seen that Paul was arrested in Jerusalem and then he went though a series of hearings in Jerusalem and Caesarea. He confronted Jewish prejudice against the Gentiles from the crowd in Jerusalem, a divided sentiment from the Sanhedrin, the deadly threat of a Jewish plot, generally considerate and protective treatment from Claudius Lysias, the ever-present motive of greed in Felix, the political cunning of Festus, and the halfway honorable treatment of Agrippa. He appealed his case to Caesar in Rome because of the impossibility of a fair hearing where he was, requiring his leaving Palestine for a lengthy sea and land voyage to the capital of the Roman Empire. Difficult and dangerous travel over inhospitable oceans would simultaneously try his faith and strengthen his resolve to serve Christ. Ahead of him in Rome would be some two years of confinement, his release from prison, and probably a second imprisonment before his eventual death for the sake of Christ.

The trip to Rome that Paul was presently beginning was one which he had mentioned, planned for, dreamed of, and prayed for. Perhaps some information concerning the prominence of this visit to Rome in the life of Paul would be helpful to us at this point of our study.

The apostle had announced his intention to go to Rome while he was in Ephesus on his third journey (Acts 19:21). As he was later receiving adamant opposition from the Jews in Jerusalem, the Lord promised him that he would bear witness in Rome (Acts 23:11). This information recorded by Luke is amplified by Paul's own writing in his Letter to the Romans. At the letter's outset the apostle spoke of his desire to visit the saints in Rome and even included such a trip in his own prayers. He did not then know how he would make it, but he prayed that it might be possible in the will of God for him to go there. He also talked about his purpose that he hoped to accomplish in Rome, as well as his being hindered from completing his earlier plans to go there (Rom. 1:10-15). Toward the end of the same letter the apostle again brought up the matter of his proposed trip to Rome. He seems to say that his personal policy of preaching the gospel where Christ was not named had kept him from visiting Rome, seemingly because he had plenty of such work where he was. As he was running out of virgin territory, he then planned to visit Rome in accord with his policy to take the message of Christ to another region. He hoped that numerous past hindrances of many years were now past so that he might travel to Rome on his way to Spain. He did mention the one remaining task that he hoped to accomplish

before setting out for Spain—delivering the collected funds to the poor among the saints in Jerusalem. To the end that he might succeed in his work in Jerusalem and safely arrive in Rome, he requested the Roman saints' prayers (Rom. 15:20-33).

It is noteworthy that all of the obstacles that arose and hopelessness of men that plagued Paul's fellow-travelers on this journey could not hinder the Lord's promise or Paul's plan from its fulfillment in this instance, for Paul's plans here accorded with God's purpose to fulfill his plans. Providence was working to achieve the Lord's will and work.

The Voyage by Sea

At the proper time, decided by the authorities no doubt, Paul was transferred to the keeping of Julius, along with some other prisoners. If these others were going to Rome to be executed, as some think was the case, Paul would have had reason for contemplating his own death; it is also possible they were going to have their cases heard by Caesar like Paul. From the centurion associated with the Emperor's Regiment (possibly one of several so named to honor the Emperor) Paul received kindness, showing that again even Gentiles often did better than Paul's own kinsmen in their treatment of him. It is also clear from his use of "we" that Luke was one of the apostle's companions to Rome, though we know nothing of his whereabouts or his involvements during Paul's two years in Caesarea. A.T. Robertson surmises that he might have been writing his account of Jesus' life during this time (*Epochs in the Life of Paul,* 254). Aristarchus, who was a Macedonian from Thessalonica, was also in Paul's company on the ship from Adramyttium (its port and its destination) as it sailed close to the coast. He had been with Paul on his third journey in Ephesus, where he had been seized (Acts 19:29) and on his return to Jerusalem (Acts 20:4-5). When Paul wrote Colossians, he called Aristarchus his fellow prisoner (Col. 4:10). The stops and other locations mentioned by Luke help us to trace the route of Paul's journey to Rome.

Evidence Convincing to a Skeptic

Author's Note: *Under my own title, I here submit an excerpt from E.A. Rowell's 1933 work* Prophecy Speaks, *published by Review and Herald Publishing Association in Tacoma Park, Washington, because of its pertinence to our present area of study in Paul's travels. The geographical accuracy of Luke's detail in recording Paul's travels was the convincing evidence in Ramsay's instance.*

Sir William Mitchell Ramsay, in 1881, was a young man of sterling integrity, unimpeachable character, culture, and high education. He had a sincere desire to know the truth. He had been educated in an atmosphere of doubt, which early brought him to the conviction that the Bible was fraudulent.

He had spent years deliberately preparing himself for the announced task of heading an exploration expedition into Asia Minor and Palestine, the home of the Bible, where he would "dig up the evidence" that the Book was the product of ambitious monks, and not the book from heaven it claimed to be. He regarded the weakest spot in the whole New Testament to be the story of Paul's travels. These had never been thoroughly investigated by one on the spot. So he announced his plan to take the book of Acts as a guide, and by trying to make the same journeys Paul made over the same routes that Paul followed, thus prove that the apostle could never have made them as he described.

. . .Equipped as no other man had been, he went to the home of the Bible. Here he spent fifteen years literally "digging for the evidence." Then in 1896 he published a large volume on *St. Paul the Traveler and the Roman Citizen.*

The book caused a furor of dismay among the skeptics of the world. Its attitude was utterly unexpected, because it was contrary to the announced intention of the author years before. The chagrin and confusion of Bible opponents was complete. But their chagrin and confusion increased, as for twenty years more, book after book from the same author came from the press, each filled with additional evidence of the exact, minute truthfulness of the whole New Testament as tested by the spade on the spot. The evidence was so overwhelming that many infidels announced their repudiation of their former unbelief and accepted Christianity. And these books have stood the test of time, not one having been refuted, nor have I found even any attempt to refute them (46-47).

The Trip over Sea

1. Sidon: This initial part of the trip covered about seventy-five miles and required a day of travel. Here Paul had special freedom from Julius to spend time with friends, who cared for him during his stay. How did Julius know that he could trust Paul to spend time away from the ship? Possibly he had learned from Festus or another military officer of Paul's trustworthiness.

2. Myra: Here the ship next touched land after slow travel for about 450 miles, resulting from opposite winds from the west during the late part of sailing season. Its path had taken it east and north of Cyprus until it came near the coast of Cilicia and Pamphylia and then farther west to Myra, a seaport in Lycia. Because the ship would continue hugging the coast until it reach its port at Adramyttium (far to the north in Asia), Julius found another ship, this one sailing for Italy, and transferred his prisoners to the second ship, which had come from Alexandria in Egypt with its cargo of grain.

3. Cnidus, Salmone: Many days of difficult travel over 130 miles brought the ship to this harbor on the southwestern tip of Asia Minor next to Rhodes and Cos and then to Cape Salmone on Crete's eastern end (125 miles from Cnidus). Contrary winds hindered the ship's entry into the port, forcing a southward turn toward Crete, "a large island (140 miles long by 35 miles wide) at the entrance to the Aegean Sea" (Pfeiffer, *Atlas* 229).

4. Fair Havens: Located about 100 miles farther around on Crete's southern side near Lasea, this port served the ship's inhabitants well for much time. Travel during the fall of the year was hazardous on the Mediterranean, accounting for the suspension of sailing from early November until early February. Luke's reference to "the Fast" tells us that the end of September and the beginning of October (the time of the Fast connected with the Day of Atonement) had passed. Sea travels then became more dangerous. It was here that Paul gave the others his personal advice, probably based on his experience on ships, that they ought to curtail travel lest they lose their lives along with the ship and its cargo. The centurion, however, placed more credence in the judgment of those men whom he judged to be the "experienced" ones and left the safe port for more perilous places. We wonder how much of the ancient Minoan and Mycenaean culture, or even Christians living here, Paul and the rest might have witnessed while here in Crete. Jews from Crete had been present in Jerusalem on Pentecost in Acts 2. Hoping to reach the better harbor for wintering fifty miles away at Phoenix, the ship sailed away to the west.

5. Clauda: Though heading for Phoenix, the ship was unable to make it because a violent "northeaster" (Euroclydon or Euroquilo, as in ASV) so strongly drove it off its course that the helmsman let the ship ride where the wind took it.

After covering twenty-five miles of its trip and reaching the shelter of the island of Clauda (Cauda in ASV) south of Crete, the sailors then took the skiff onto the ship with difficulty and also strengthened the ship by wrapping ropes around it.

Across the open Mediterranean the violent winds carried the ship for two weeks, creating fear of running aground on the Syrtis Sands and causing attempts to lighten the ship's load by jettisoning some of its cargo. The people on the ship lost their hope for escaping the storm's wrath after many days of this tempest without food in the deep under a darkened sky, but Paul told them of a hopeful message that God's angel had delivered to him to assure the deliverance of all on the ship. Paul's faith was grounded in God, so that he feared no loss of life but conceded the loss of the ship as it would run aground on an island.

> **Travel during the fall of the year was hazardous on the Mediterranean, accounting for the suspension of sailing from early November till early February.**

6. Melita (Malta): As the ship neared this island, located about 480 miles to the west from Clauda, after being driven by the wind for fourteen days, the experienced sailors thought they were near land, possibly from hearing or seeing the effect of the breakers formed on the northeast side of the island. St. Paul's Bay is the modern name of the bay where Paul and others found land. This section of the Mediterranean Sea between Crete and Malta, as well as the water separating Italy and the Grecian peninsula, then bore the name of the Sea of Adria.

When soundings revealed that they were getting closer to land, they dropped four anchors to secure their position until daylight came.

During darkness some sailors tried to escape by means of the skiff onto the island. Paul warned that they must stay on the ship to escape death, and the soldiers cut the small boat loose.

drop into the water, loosed the rudder ropes, and raised the mainsail to the wind. Here they ran the ship aground where two seas met, causing the forepart of the ship to stick to the point of being immovable

hand. The superstitious natives thought this showed Paul was a criminal, but they later thought him a god because he suffered no harm from the snake. For three months the ship's inhabitants remained on Malta, with at least Paul and Luke being received by the chief man of the island—Publius—for three days. Paul healed Publius' father and others while there. It is highly unlikely that the apostle here performed miracles merely for their own physical purpose of healing, for such he never had done before. We then conclude there was teaching of the gospel here, and the miracles served as verifications of the messenger's credibility. History does not indicate clearly the existence of a church here until the fifth century A.D., though Christian influence in the art of this island is found as early as the second century. As they departed in another Alexandrian ship, the people of the island sent them on their way with things needed for the trip. The dangerous travel conditions having passed during their winter on Malta, the ship left for the mainland of Italy on the way to Rome.

> **It is highly unlikely that the apostle here performed miracles merely for their own physical purpose of healing, for such he never had done before. We then conclude there was teaching of the gospel here, and the miracles served as verifications of the messenger's credibility.**

Just as day was dawning, Paul urged all to eat food for their survival, since they had gone without for fourteen days. Paul's own example of eating, after he had thanked God for his goodness, encouraged the rest of the 276 passengers on the ship to eat. They then lightened the ship by throwing wheat into the sea.

When it was day they did not recognize the land where they had wrecked. In order to run the ship onto the beach forming the bay which they saw, they let the anchors

and the rear part to break apart from the fierce waves. The soldiers then wanted to kill all prisoners to prevent their escape; but the centurion instructed them to swim or float on boards to the land, out of special kindness to Paul. By these means all of them escaped safely to land.

Once on the island, they learned from the friendly natives that the island was named Malta. In cold and rainy weather the natives provided them a fire, out of which a viper came to fasten on Paul's

7. Syracuse: The trip to the mainland would first take Paul to this city on the largest island (Sicily) in the Mediterranean Sea, located 110 miles to the north from Malta and 100 miles south from the toe of Italy's boot. Here the ship from Alexandria, bearing the sign of the Twin Brothers (Castor and Pollux), two pagan gods and "sons of Zeus," to whom seamen looked for help, docked for three days. The heathenism of the ship's owners thus overshadowed the blessing from the living and true God in delivering the ship's 276 inhabitants from the storm.

8. Rhegium (modern Reggio di Calabria—Pfeiffer, 230): A circu-

As Paul came into Rome, he would have traveled along the Appian Way parts of which still remain.

itous route (indicated in the renderings of ASV, NASV, and NKJB) brought the ship some 100 miles northward. Here Paul and his company stayed one day until the favorable south wind accommodated the ship's northward journey.

The Trip over Land

1. Puteoli (modern Pozzuoli, eight miles east of Naples—Pfeiffer 230): From this point some 200 miles to the north on the western coast of Italy, the travel would proceed over land to Rome, situated 141 miles away. What a joy and comfort it must have been to Paul and the other Christians to find brethren, who invited them to stay for seven days. Repeated leniency from Julius had been the rule on this trip, and this stop was no exception. Though the apostle might have had the company of a guard, he still was able to meet with the Lord's disciples on the Lord's Day to eat the Lord's supper.

2. Apii Forum and Three Inns: Luke especially marks their departure from Puteoli, "And so we went toward Rome" (Acts 28:14). At both of these locations, brethren who had heard from Rome of the approaching party came to greet them. These places were located along the famous Appian Way, forty miles and thirty miles, respectively, from Rome, the latter of them being a usual way-station for travelers. Paul thanked God for their presence and took courage from them.

3. Rome: Paul's final leg of this journey of some 1,936 miles must have been easier than the first part, because he enjoyed the memory of God's blessing throughout the trip and the accompaniment of Christians who had come to salute him. In the care of God and his people, Paul was able to rest comfortably, though his body might have shown

The Roman Coliseum was the sight of many gladiator contests and at least some persecution of Christians.

the wear and fatigue of travel. Another reason for his more abundant joy was his realizations of his plans and God's providence after many years. Many think that the trip took place from the fall of A.D. 60 to the spring of 61.

Paul's Confinement in Rome

Luke tells us that Paul's imprisonment in Rome lasted two years, which we judge to have been from A.D. 61 to 63. No one acquainted with Paul's life as a Christian will be surprised to learn of his busy and active work while a prisoner. In addition to the work here described by Luke, the apostle also wrote four of his epistles from Rome. We often hear or speak of his "prison epistles"—Colossians, Ephesians, Philemon, and Philippians.

Pfeiffer (*Atlas,* 230) informs us that Rome covered ten hills and their intervening valleys, as well as a plain along the Tiber River. Its population was approximately 1,200,000 at this time, of whom about half were slaves and a large percentage of the other half were paupers supported in their idleness

by free food and the games at a sports complex called Circus Maximus, with seating estimates from 135,000 people to 200,000 (Barnes 59; Jenkins, 90). Present also were the palaces of the Caesars on the Palatine Hill, the Temple of Castor and Pollux serving as a kind of "bureau of weights and measures," the Roman Forum, the "hub of Roman life—religious, political, economic, social (Jenkins 88), the Coliseum (holding 80,000), public baths, and the catacombs (587 miles of passages/rooms under the city).

In Rome the centurion delivered Paul to the captain of the guard, but the apostle in chains enjoyed relative freedom in his rented house with a soldier as his guard. Burrus is traditionally known as the Praetorian Prefect in this instance, though Ramsay disputes this in his book on Paul's travels. Luke no more uses his typical "we" to designate his presence with Paul after he had to part company with the prisoner.

Paul's first order of business in Rome was to call Jewish leaders to meet with him to explain his presence in Rome, resulting from protests of Jews against his innocent behavior and their insistence on his guilt, even to the point of his having to appeal to Caesar. The Jews in Rome, claiming to know nothing of his case, asked for an opportunity to hear him concerning his hope (identified by Paul as the hope of Israel) as part of a much maligned sect. Whether their ignorance resulted from indifference or fear of embarrassment of Jerusalem Jews, difficulty of sending information, or divine providence, we know not; but their absence in Rome probably worked to Paul's advantage. Paul the preacher was working under adverse conditions, but he was mindful of their souls.

On the appointed day many Jews came to Paul's lodging to hear him explain about God's kingdom and persuade concerning Jesus from the Law and the Prophets from morning till evening. Some be-lieved but others did not. Paul's final word to them related to Isaiah's prophecy concerning the hardened hearts of many hearing the word and the extension of the gospel to more fair-minded Gentiles; the Jews who disagreed with each other over Paul's teaching disputed further over this final word, leaving Paul in fulfillment of the very words that he had spoken from the prophet.

Paul enjoyed liberty to teach confidently all who came to visit him for the next two years. At some point he converted Onesimus to Jesus Christ (Phile. 10). Various helpers spent time with Paul and aided him during this time (Luke—Acts 28:16; Timothy—Phile. 1; Col. 1:1; Epaphras—Phile. 23; Col. 1:3-8; 4:12-13; Onesimus—Phile. 11; Tychicus—Col. 4:7-9; Eph. 6:21-22; Marcus, Aristarchus, Demas, Luke, and Jesus/Justus—Phile. 24; Col. 4:10-14; Epaphroditus—Phil. 2:25-30; 4:18, 22). It is clear that God's word was not then bound, as he declared in 2 Timothy 2:9. The confident zeal of the Lord's apostle and the power of the gospel are abundantly evident during this time in his life.

Paul's joy in trial was also manifest in so much of his writing during this time. It would be helpful for students to read of Paul's imprisonment, as reflected in his prison letters (Col. 4:2-4; Eph. 3:1; 4:10; 6:18-20; Phile. 8-9; Phil. 1:7, 12-16). Paul expected to be released (Phil. 1:23-27; Phile. 22). At this point Luke stops his account of Paul's life.

From various clues found in the New Testament, we believe that his release did come and that he spent some years in freedom, only to be confined again. The next lesson will consider this period in Paul's life.

Define These Words as Used in Relation to Paul's Life

1. Julius: _____

2. Emperor's Regiment: _____

3. The Fast: _____

4. Euroclydon: _____

5. Melita (Malta): _____

6. Publius: _____

7. Twin Brothers: _____

8. Onesimus: _____

Discussion Questions

1. Discuss the various trials faced by Paul between his arrest in Jerusalem and his Roman trial._____

    _____

    _____

2. What had Paul said and written about going to Rome in Acts and Romans? _____

    _____

3. Show from this trip Paul's enjoyment of time spent with brethren._____
_____

4. Cite different occasions of kindness shown Paul by Julius._____
_____
_____

5. In what way did Apii Forum and Three Inns provide special joy to Paul? _____
_____

6. Tell something about the Rome of Paul's day. _____
_____
_____

7. Describe Paul's teaching to those Jews coming to hear him in Rome. _____
_____

8. What did Paul mean by "the hope of Israel," for which he was a prisoner? _____
_____
_____

9. Use Paul's four prison letters to show the following: (a) Paul's state of mind, (b) his helpers, and (c) his expectation of release. _____
_____
_____
_____

Paul's Final Years

If we accept the close of Acts of the Apostles as anticipating the imminent end of Paul's life, we have some major difficulties in explaining various passages found in some of his letters, especially those to Timothy and Titus. While it is possible that his life soon ended after Luke's account of his two-year stay in Rome, it does not seem very likely in view of some enigmatic statements to which we just alluded. It will be our intent in this lesson to explore some of these statements and derive possible explanations for them in the light of what we know of Paul's life.

Important Passages to Consider

But I trust in the Lord that I myself shall also come shortly. Yet I considered it necessary to send to you Epaphroditus, my brother, fellow worker, and fellow soldier, but your messenger and the one who ministered to my need (Phil. 2:24-25).

But, meanwhile, also prepare a guest room for me, for I trust that through your prayers I shall be granted to you (Phile. 1:22).

As I urged you when I went into Macedonia—remain in Ephesus that you may charge some that they teach no other doctrine (1 Tim. 1:3).

These things I write to you, though I hope to come to you shortly; but if I am delayed, I write so that you may know how you ought to conduct yourself in the house of God, which is the church of the living God, the pillar and ground of the truth (1 Tim. 3:14-15).

For this reason I left you in Crete, that you should set in order the things that are lacking, and appoint elders in every city as I commanded you (Tit. 1:5).

When I send Artemas to you, or Tychicus, be diligent to come to me at Nicopolis, for I have decided to spend the winter there (Tit. 3:12).

And because the harbor was not suitable to winter in, the majority advised to set sail from there also, if by any means they could reach Phoenix, a harbor of Crete opening toward the southwest and northwest, and winter there (Acts 27:12).

Erastus stayed in Corinth, but Trophimus I have left in Miletus sick (2 Tim. 4:20).

And Sopater of Berea accompanied him to Asia—also Aristarchus and Secundus of the Thessalonians, and Gaius of Derbe, and Timothy, and Tychicus and Trophimus of Asia (Acts 20:4).

From Miletus he sent to Ephesus and called for the elders of the church (Acts 20:17).

(For they had previously seen Trophimus the Ephesian with him in the city, whom they supposed that Paul had brought into the temple) (Acts 21:29).

Bring the cloak that I left with Carpus at Troas when you come—and the books, especially the parchments (2 Tim. 4:13).

For I am already being poured out as a drink offering, and the time of my departure is at hand (2 Tim. 4:6).

Paul's Account/Plans in Relation to Luke's Account

Close examination of these passages discloses some differences between what Paul did or planned to do and what Luke reported about Paul in Acts. The differences that come to light are noticeable, because in some case they are the very opposite of what Luke says in Acts, so that it is reasonable to conclude that Paul's record relates to some different times and circumstances after the close of Acts. The student is urged to think about the following variations in the accounts:

1. When Paul wrote to Philippi from prison in Rome (Phil. 2:24-27), the Christians there had known of his need and also sent Epaphroditus to help him in his need. They also had learned of the latter's sickness and expressed concern over him. While sending him to them, Paul makes it clear that he plans to come to see them soon. From this letter we learn that Paul hoped soon to be a free man.

2. We also learn from Philemon 10 that Paul converted Philemon's slave Onesimus, who was from Colossae (Col. 4:9), meaning that his master was also from that town. In his Letter to Philemon, Paul asks him to prepare a place for him to lodge when he came (Phile. 22). This statement provides additional evidence that the apostle expected

and desired to be released soon. It would seem plausible that Paul is writing of circumstances later than Luke's account in Acts and indicates the more hopeful situation then existing.

3. In Paul's First Letter to Timothy, he speaks of leaving Timothy in Ephesus on the apostle's trip to Macedonia so the young preacher could deal with false teachers and with some pressing needs in the church there, indicating his hope to join him soon (1:3; 3:14-15). In Luke's account of the third journey in 19:22, it was Paul staying in Ephesus and Timothy going to Macedonia. When Paul finally went to Macedonia after the riot in Ephesus and wrote the Second Letter to Corinth, Timothy was there with the apostle (2 Cor. 1:1). In this analysis of passages we see a different time being described in the two accounts of Luke and Paul.

4. In Titus we learn of Paul's leaving Titus in Crete to set in order the churches by appointing elders (1:5), as he traveled freely. On his trip to Rome as a prisoner he stopped on Crete without Titus, evidently, in that he is not mentioned (Acts 27:12). Paul further wrote asking Titus to join him in Nicopolis (3:12). Luke's record at the end of Acts does not provide a framework into which Paul's later travels can fit.

5. When the apostle wrote to Timothy the second time, he mentioned that Erastus stayed in Corinth (4:20), evidently because Timothy was not there to know about such. On Paul's third journey Timothy was present with Paul in Corinth (Acts 20:1-4).

6. Again in 2 Timothy 4:20 Paul says that he left an ill Trophimus in Miletus, but Luke's account in Acts 20:17 has Trophimus traveling with Paul through Miletus and on to

Jerusalem, where some of the Jews saw him and falsely accused Paul of bringing Greeks into the Temple to defile it (21:28-29).

7. Observe the contrast between Paul's earlier hope for his release in his writings to Philemon and the Philippians with his realization that the pouring out of himself as a drink offering had already begun in 2 Timothy 4:6.

In the seven specific situations just presented, it grows increasingly clear that Luke and Paul are describing times/situations that are quite different from one another. Luke's record in the closing chapter

of Acts takes the apostle's life up to a certain point and leaves him a prisoner, whereas Paul later provides additional information about the last few years of his life of freedom to travel and work again, his subsequent re-arrest, and his awaiting his death. As Luke closes his record, we have the portrait of this courageous hero of the faith calmly awaiting his trial before Caesar and using the opportunity for the cause of the gospel. He wrote nothing more because those events had not then taken place. Paul was later able to give a more complete record of what transpired following the close of Luke's inspired narrative. We will look later at that record and the events there sparsely chronicled.

Possible Evidence From Hebrews

We do not present this evidence with the same certainty that characterizes that presented earlier, for

we do not know definitely that Paul authored the Epistle to the Hebrews. Christians during the early centuries sometimes spoke of his authorship, however. There is some existing evidence in the letter itself to that effect. If the letter did come from Paul's pen, then the following information is highly relevant to this study; for this reason we do not disregard it. In Hebrews 13:23-24 there is evidence that Paul was in Italy and expected to leave there with Timothy upon his release to visit the recipients of his letter.

Know that our brother Timothy has been set free, with whom I shall see you if he comes shortly.

In the seven specific situations just presented, it grows increasingly clear that Luke and Paul are describing times/situations that are quite different from one another.

Greet all those who rule over you, and all the saints. Those from Italy greet you (Heb. 13:23-24).

No Trial in Acts

It seems unlikely that Paul's trial had happened before Luke finished his record in Acts 28, especially in view of his clear and detailed account of the apostle's other trials/hearings all the way from Jerusalem to Rome. Neither Felix nor Festus had found evidence that would have kept Paul a prisoner. The clear presumption of Luke's account was that he would be freed, and the clear thinking of Paul that we have already noted was that he would be freed. Any doubt about his release disappears when the evidence from Paul's own hand gains a fair hearing.

Paul's Circumstances During His Confinement

We learn something of the

apostle's life during the two years in Rome from various writings available to us. In Acts we learn that Paul spent two years receiving those who wished to visit him and teaching them of Christ. From his prison epistles we learn of some who were his companions during this time—Tychicus and Onesimus. The former of these took the epistles to the Christians in Ephesus and Colossae (Eph. 6:21-22; Col. 4:7-9), and the latter took the one to Philemon (Phile. 10-12). The reader should recall others who were present with Paul during his confinement from Lesson 11.

We also gather from Paul's writings that there were some hindrances to his teaching, even to his own personal boldness in speaking the message of Christ.

> Praying always with all prayer and supplication in the Spirit, being watchful to this end with all perseverance and supplication for all the saints— and for me, that utterance may be given to me, that I may open my mouth boldly to make known the mystery of the gospel (Eph 6:18-19).

> Continue earnestly in prayer, being vigilant in it with thanksgiving; meanwhile praying also for us, that God would open to us a door for the word, to speak the mystery of Christ, for which I am also in chains, that I may make it manifest, as I ought to speak (Col 4:2-4).

In these passages the reader is able to discern some concern on Paul's part for an occasion to teach the gospel. He evidently also personally needed their prayers for him to be bold in his teaching, possibly in view of obstacles that might have discouraged, intimidated, or even frightened him.

In the Letter to Philemon we learn of Paul's involvement in teaching a runaway slave, Onesimus, during this confinement and sending him back to his master, though he would have benefited from keeping him as his helper.

The Epistle to the Philippians, written a little later during his imprisonment, shows that Paul the prisoner had opportunity to teach some in the palace guard and to embolden some of his brethren by his own boldness in his chains (Phil. 1:12-14). What divine wisdom was evident in the circumstances allowing Paul to be where he was so that he might teach some to whom he earlier would have had no access. What wisdom Paul demonstrated in his recognition of his need for strength and boldness and in his request for the brethren's prayers on his behalf.

What Happened After His Release?

Though the New Testament nowhere directly declares the scenario that we here present, it is manifest that the plans and events earlier connected to Paul's final years simply do not fit into the earlier history of his life found in Acts or his own epistles. They do pertain to the later years of Paul, following his release from Roman imprisonment. Various explanations have been given (the reader might wish to consult Thomas on his release and Conybeare and Howson on these travels), but J.W. McGarvey's arrangement of the events is given here (*Commentary on Acts*, 296):

> He first fulfilled the purpose so confidently expressed to the Philippians of visiting them again (Phil. 2:24) and next took advantage of the lodging which he had directed Philemon to prepare for him at Colosse (Phile. 22). While in Asia he would scarcely pass by the city of Ephesus; but it is after a short visit to Spain that we locate that visit, at the conclusion of which he left Timothy there and went into Macedonia. It was contrary to the expectation once entertained by Paul, that he was once more greeted by the brethren in Ephesus; for he had bidden them farewell four years ago with the conviction that they would see his face no more (Acts 20:25). Leaving Timothy in Ephesus, and going to Macedonia, he wrote back to him the First Epistle to Timothy (1 Tim. 1:3), in which he expressed a hope of rejoining him soon at Ephesus (1 Tim. 3:14). This he most likely did, as he soon after visited Crete, in company with Titus; and the most usual route from Macedonia to this island was by way of Ephesus. Having made a short visit to Crete, he left Titus there, to "set in order the things that were wanting and to ordain elders in every city" (Tit. 1:5). Shortly after leaving the island he wrote the Epistle to Titus. He was then on his way to Nicopolis, a city of Epirus, where he expected to spend the winter (Tit. 3:12). On the way he had passed through Miletus where he had left Trophimus sick; and Corinth, where he left Erastus (2 Tim. 4:20). Whether he spent the entire winter in Nicopolis, or was imprisoned again before spring, is not certainly known; but the next that we know of him, he was a prisoner in Rome a second time, as is indicated in his Second Epistle to Timothy. From this epistle we learn certain interesting particulars of his last imprisonment, and of the beginning of his final trial. His situation was more alarming, and he was attended by fewer friends than before. Demas forsook him, through love of the world, and went to Thessalonica; Crescens, for some reason unexplained, went to Galatia, and Titus to Dalmatia (2 Tim. 4:10). Tychicus he had sent to Ephesus (2 Tim. 4:12). Luke alone, of all his former fellow-

Great Bible Characters: Paul

laborers, was with him, though he was expecting Timothy to soon rejoin him, and bring Mark with him (2 Tim. 4:11).

During his latter imprisonment in Rome, there were evidently two phases of the trial—the first, when no man stood by his side to support him and a later one (2 Tim. 4:16-17). This is likely the occasion when "Alexander the coppersmith did me much harm" (2 Tim. 4:14). Whether he was the same Alexander as the one in Acts 19 or not, this probable accuser had hurt Paul's cause. The mention of his preaching to Gentiles in 2 Timothy 4:17 probably indicates the sizeable gathering of people present at the hearing to see and hear the most noted Christian of that day. Paul does write that the Lord stood with him to strengthen him for his preaching, with the result of his deliverance from the mouth of the lion. Paul probably here compared his situation to that of Daniel in the den of lions, when an angel closed the lions' mouths to prevent harm to God's prophet (Dan. 6).

The Mamertine Prison in Rome is thought to be where Paul was imprisoned prior to his execution by the Roman government.

finished the race, I have kept the faith. Finally, there is laid up for me the crown of righteousness, which the Lord, the righteous Judge, will give to me on that Day, and not to me only but also to all who have loved His appearing (2 Tim. 4:6-8).

He had served him for many years and soon he would be able see him who appeared to Paul on his earlier journey to persecute disciples of Jesus. Because that first journey had ended short of its objective, Paul was now able to rejoice in the hope of this later journey. Paul's use of "departure"—*analuseōs*—suggests the metaphor of a trip or of breaking camp and is comparable to his dying (Phil. 1:23). Tradition says that Paul was beheaded on the Ostian Road near Rome, in keeping with Rome's practice of executing prominent criminals away from the city to avoid crowds (Robertson, 316, ISBE 2287). Paul's glorious end—glorious retrospectively, introspectively, and prospectively—stands in vivid contrast with the inglorious end of the current emperor Nero, who committed suicide (Keller, 346). He took that final journey sometime between A.D. 66 and 68, but before departing he had given to the world a valuable section of the New Testament. Our final lesson will consider Paul as a writer of many New Testament books.

> **Tradition says that Paul was beheaded on the Ostian Road near Rome, in keeping with Rome's practice of executing prominent criminals away from the city to avoid crowds.**

To the second phase of his trial the apostle evidently pointed, with the realization that its outcome would be his death, when he spoke of his already being offered (2 Tim. 4:6). Read again his happy anticipation of that final journey on which he soon would embark:

For I am already being poured out as a drink offering, and the time of my departure is at hand. I have fought the good fight, I have

The second part of the trial came after his likely wait in the Mamertine Prison, or at some place with military guard.

Paul's Glorious End

Paul seemed to have little time left on earth and little to which he could look forward, but his outlook was bright, for his heavenly reward would be everlasting in the company of his Savior and King.

Define These Terms as Used in Relation to Paul's Life

1. Epaphroditus: _____

2. Onesimus: _____

3. Nicopolis: _____

4. Trophimus: _____

5. Philemon: _____

6. A.D. 66-68: _____

Discussion Questions

1. What evidence is there that Tychicus probably delivered the epistles to Ephesus and Colossae? _____
_____

2. Cite some instances of variations between Luke's account in Acts and Paul's account in his epistles. _____
_____

3. How much weight should be given to the evidence in Hebrews 13? _____
_____

4. Is it reasonable to conclude that Paul's trial had not taken place before Luke ended his inspired record? Why?
_____
_____

5. Can you think of a better arrangement of these events in Paul's last years than the one McGarvey presented?
_____

6. Why is it possible to describe the end of the apostle's life as glorious? _____
_____

7. What can each person do to assure his own end of life is similarly glorious? _____
_____

8. What similarities and differences can you think of between Paul's trip to Damascus and his final trip to be with the Lord? _____
_____

Paul—Major Contributor to the New Testament

The chief reason why many do not understand some of the more difficult sections of the Bible is their failure to comprehend the situation from which the writing arose. What is true of the Bible generally is also true of the writings of Paul. Within the bounds of space available, it will be our plan in this lesson to present some information which will aid the student in understanding the letters first in their local situations. It is not our intent to delve into the genuineness or authenticity of the letters or the justification for their inclusion in the New Testament.

Paul gave us more than one-fourth of the New Testament—fourteen letters, one hundred of its chapters—when we include Hebrews, which we here take to be from his pen. Like other books, Paul's letters are there because they could not be kept out. Their evidence of inspiration and canonicity is clear to the honest student, when comparison is made with the spurious gospels and false epistles. Passing of time and evidence of their apostolic connection decided in their favor, leaving so-called church councils only to recognize them as accredited divine revelation from Paul.

This lesson will demonstrate that Paul's concern for his brethren, his daily care for all the churches (2 Cor. 11:28) and for particular brethren, did not cease with his converting people, forming congregations, or merely sending someone else to help them, but extended to his involvement through messengers, intermediaries, personal visits, and his letters. It will also help to show that the principles given by the Holy Spirit to guide congregations and Christians to solve their problems in the first century are applicable to our problems in the twenty-first century because of their timelessness.

The effect of Paul's work in the Gentile world was colossal, for he not only converted many of the Gentile Christians but also changed the thinking of the Jewish Christians toward the Gentiles in large measure. By the time of his death there had been a major transition in concept from a kingdom for the Jews to one for all people. Such a development should not ignore

> **The effect of Paul's work in the Gentile world was colossal, for he not only converted many of the Gentile Christians but also changed the thinking of the Jewish Christians toward the Gentiles in large measure.**

Christ's part, nor should it disregard the role of this "apostle to the Gentiles." Paul's words of sober truth deserve our consideration: ". . .but I labored more abundantly than they all, yet not I, but the grace of God which was in me" (1 Cor. 15:10).

Paul's Epistles From the Second Journey (ca. A.D. 53)

The dates assigned to the four groups of epistles (placed at each heading) are approximate and general for the group, because in the case of the two Thessalonian letters in this group, actually 52 and 53 are the more likely years when Paul

wrote **1 and 2 Thessalonians**. After the beleaguered beginning of the gospel and the church in Thessalonica in Acts 17 (1 Thess. 1:6; 2:2), a concerned Paul went on to Berea and then Athens, where he finally sent Timothy to learn of their state and bring him a report (1 Thess. 3:1-7). After Paul reached Corinth, Timothy arrived with assuring news about the faith of the saints there and their desire for Paul's return. He then wrote **1 Thessalonians** to put to rest rumors circulated concerning his motives in earlier preaching there (1 Thess. 2:1-12), and to remove their false ideas of the hopeless state of their deceased brothers and sisters upon the Lord's return (4:13-18), being careful to connect their hope to the second coming in each of the five chapters (1:10; 2:19; 3:13; 4:13-18; 5:1-11, 23). He gave further instruction to cease their idleness (4:9-12), to correct their misuse of miraculous gifts (5:19-20), and to show more caution over the influence of the evil of paganism (5:21-22).

In Paul's **Second Epistle to the Thessalonians**, Paul must have heard about them from some messenger, because we find Paul responding to a letter claiming to have been from him (2 Thess. 2:2). He now writes a few months later about their excitement over the coming of the Lord, about which he had written in the first epistle. Some of them had apparently misunderstood him to mean that Christ was then about to come immediately (2 Thess. 2:1-2), and they had allowed this state

misunderstandings and directing their faith in obedience to Christ.

Paul's Epistles From the Third Journey (ca. A.D. 58)

First and Second Corinthians, Galatians, and Romans came forth from the apostle's Third Missionary Journey close to the year A.D. 58. Most of them manifest the same doctrinal concern regarding justification by deeds of the Law, because they deal with similar situations arising in different areas where Paul had traveled and gained influence. Paul had proclaimed the gospel of

over their different leaders, their arrogance in the midst of a moral scandal, problems among brethren not handled properly, and their inclination to abuse their liberty in Christ (chapters 1-6)—and their concerns in the letter—questions about marriage and its problems, meats sacrificed to idols, women and their veils, the Lord's supper, spiritual gifts, the resurrection of the dead, and the collection for the saints (chapters 7-16). In this epistle we probably have the most diverse of all New Testament epistles, providing us an insight into the actual functioning of the Corinthian congregation, both commendable and condemnable, and an opportunity to "remove the roof from the meeting-places of the early Christians and look inside" (Thomas, 29), with no letter granting a better opportunity that 1 Corinthians.

> In this epistle we probably have the most diverse of all New Testament epistles, providing us an insight into the actual functioning of the Corinthian congregation, both commendable and condemnable, and an opportunity to "remove the roof from the meeting-places of the early Christians and look inside."

of expectancy to affect their work habits, inducing the spirit of idleness/slothfulness (3:6-15). He assured them that there would first be a falling away from faithfulness to Christ before the Lord would come (2:3). Paul also obviously had some concern about their being drawn away from the apostolic traditions, possibly in their assembly (2:15). It is interesting that Paul's motivation to them to stand fast was God's work of redemption, begun before the world began, accomplished by the Spirit's sanctification in collaboration with their belief of the truth ("two sides of the same coin"), effected by the call of God in the gospel, and culminating in their eternal glory with Jesus Christ (2:13-14). The second letter then became an important means of adjusting their

Christ in Corinth, where "Greek religion implemented and channelized sensual vices, commercializing them under the guise of worship" (Thomas, 23-24). After he left there to complete his second journey and begin his third one, leading him to stay three years in Ephesus, matters developed unsatisfactorily in the congregation in Corinth.

After learning of their problems from some of Corinth's members (1 Cor. 1:11; 16:17-18) and receiving questions in a letter from them (1 Cor. 7:1), which some believe was their response to an unsaved letter implied in 5:9, Paul wrote his **First Epistle to the Corinthians**, probably in the spring of A.D. 57 (1 Cor. 16:8). In the First Epistle Paul dealt with their problems about which he had heard—their contentions

The reception of Paul's first epistle was satisfactory among a majority of the Christians in Corinth (2 Cor. 1-7); but there was a distinct minority, led by some influential person, which seemed to intensify its radical opposition to Paul (ch. 10-13; 11:4). Paul probably responded to the news of this division in sentiment toward him, learned from Titus in Ephesus or Philippi (2:12-13; 7:5-7), by writing the **Second Epistle to the Corinthians** later the same year as the first letter, or early in A.D. 58. The second letter varies widely in its portrait of Paul's moods, emotions, boldness, and language, because it deals with such opposite responses to his first letter, causing some to insist that his second epistle is the most nearly autobiographical writing that Paul has given us. In the second epistle we find that the response of the minority was one of questioning/charging Paul concerning his personal appearance, speech, authority, teaching, character, and probably even his apostleship. Paul's response to these charges came in the form of his vindication of his ministry (chapters 1-7) and his personal defense (chapters 10-13), separated by a section concerning the contribution that he had earlier told them about (chapters 8-9). Such diversity of subject matter makes for the most puzzling, emotional, and personal letter which comes from Paul.

Because of their similar theme, expounded more and in more detail in the Roman letter, both Galatians and Romans have long been considered to have been written about the same time and possibly from the same place to deal with somewhat the same problems. Romans 15:19-28 indicates that Paul had already collected the contributions of various congregations, including that of Corinth, where he probably was then writing, and was soon to depart for Jerusalem to bring the bounty to aid the poor among the saints there. Because the Epistle to the Romans is a more detailed and weighty treatise, many think the apostle wrote it after his earlier brief personal letter sent to the Galatian churches. In keeping with our indications of previous lessons, Paul wrote his **Epistle to the Galatians** in the latter part of A.D. 57 and the **Epistle to the Romans** in the early part of A.D. 58, because of Luke's mention of both Passover (March-April) and Pentecost (May-June) as touching on his plan for travel from Corinth to Jerusalem in Acts 20:6, 16.

In his letter to the Galatians, Paul's abrupt beginning with a strong reprimand for the desertion of Christ among the Galatians is different from most of his other letters. His initial severe language and tone seem to grow stronger as he continues to respond to the work of the Judaizers in attacking his character and his apostleship. He stoutly maintains the liberty of Christians under the gospel to serve Christ, not their enslavement under the Law's bondage. His independence as an apostle from the other apostles, the revelation of his message from the Lord rather than its coming from the rest of the apostles, the preeminence of the gospel over the Law, Paul's consistent teaching/behavior in relation to such matters of the Law as circumcision, and the life of righteousness emanating from the Spirit as superior to the legal ceremonies and observances of Moses are themes that penetrate the letter.

> **Because of their similar theme, expounded more and in more detail in the Roman letter, both Galatians and Romans have long been considered to have been written about the same time and possibly from the same place to deal with somewhat the same problems.**

The content of the letter leads us to believe that the same infectious leaven of wickedness was working among the Galatians as among the Corinthians, as seen in Paul's second letter to them.

While mostly present in the Roman letter as well (because the workers of evil were already at work or soon would arrive), these same themes are there more elaborately, fully, and formally woven into the tapestry of the overlying message of gospel superiority. Both letters share the same view of the relation of the dispensation of Moses to the entire scheme of human redemption and the attainment of righteousness (justification before God) by means of the gospel of Christ, in contrast to the meritorious deeds of the Law. The theme

of Paul's writing to the Romans appears early in 1:16-17, to be developed fully in later chapters. His initial point is that all people, Jews and Gentiles alike, need the righteousness revealed in the gospel because of the universality of sin (chapters 1-3). The gospel also provides the benefits of that righteousness (justification) obtained by the sacrificial death of Jesus Christ and attained in union with Christ by baptism into him, in the likeness of his death and resurrection (chs. 5-8). One section of the letter addresses the problem raised by the Jews who thought God had cast off the people whom he had earlier chosen (chs. 9-11). Practical matters, including the relation between the Jew and the Gentile over long standing practices relating to days and meats, gain Paul's attention in chapters 12-15.

Paul's Epistles From the First Roman Imprisonment (ca. A.D. 63)

Four epistles from Paul's confinement in Rome can justly be styled his "prison epistles"—Philemon, Colossians, Ephesians, and Philippians. All of them contain reference to his being a prisoner (Phile. 1:9, 13, 23; Col. 4:18; Eph. 3:1; 4:l; Phil. 1:13, 17), but after this common feature the close student notices that the first three letters differ much from the Philippian letter. It appears that Philippians came later (some say earlier) than the other three letters, because of the absence of Luke from the letter (and from Paul's company), while two letters imply the doctor's presence in Rome when the first three were written (Phile. 1:24; Col. 4:14). A comparison of Philemon 1:10-12 with Colossians 4:7-9 suggests that Paul sent both letters in the company of Onesimus; moreover, both Ephesians 6:21 and Colossians 4:7 seem to place Tychicus in that same company in delivering the two letters.

In the **Epistle to Philemon**, the only personal letter of Paul, Paul elevates the value of even a slave—in this case Onesimus, whom the apos-

with it (2:3, 8); (2) the ritualism of the Law of Moses, still held by some (2:11-17); (3) the worship of angels, a practice that was later part of Gnosticism (2:18); and (4) self-imposed rules of asceticism (2:20-23). Paul hit this speculative Greek-Jewish doctrine head-on by employing the very vocabulary used and associating its claimed strengths with the superior way of Jesus Christ—"knowledge," "fullness," and "mystery." The heresy probably had not advanced to the full blown Gnosticism later associated with this area in the second century, but its incipient strains were evident by now. We have the advantage of Paul's inspired teaching about

receives special focus in this letter, even as Christ did in the Colossian letter. It is possible that this letter was a "circular letter," intended for general use among different churches, including Laodicea, because of no personal greetings found in the letter and because of Paul's reference to a letter to Laodicea in Colossians 4:13-16. It does seem quite strange that Paul would include no greeting and mention no names in Ephesus in his letter after working there longer (three years) than in any other location.

The **Epistle to the Philippians** drew on the humility of Christ to urge such lowliness upon them in their striving for the faith of the gospel. Different times in this letter Paul either appealed for their being of the same mind or shows them how to attain it through such humility (1:27-30; 2:1-11; 4:1-3). He also assured them of his love and gratitude for their past help and of his present welfare, showing also the progress of the gospel in the Praetorian Guard during his imprisonment (1:3-26; 4:10-18). He further wrote extensively concerning both Timothy and Epaphroditus, helpful workers to Paul and to the brethren (2:19-30). He warned them about some teachers advocating a return to the Law (3:1-11) and a freedom from the restraints of law/antinomianism (3:12-4:1). Through all of his personal problems and those of the Philippians, the joy of serving Christ stands out brilliantly as a key-note of this letter. From the prison in Philippi to the prison in Rome, Paul's joy in the Lord, which is the Christian's strength (Neh. 8:10), is undeniable and unforgettable. Possibly a year or so later than the other prison letters (A.D. 63-64), because of the time allowing for the progress of teaching among the Praetorian Guard and the mak-

> **We have the advantage of Paul's inspired teaching about Christ's nature and role in this most detailed explanation of such matters found in the New Testament.**

tle had turned to Christ during his imprisonment—in the affairs of the church, as he sent him back to his master with instructions concerning the master's behavior toward his returned slave and the slave's toward his master, knowing that both of them served the same Master.

The **Epistle to the Colossians**, possibly written after Paul's learning from Epaphras of the heresy in the church there (Col. 1:7-9; 4:12), described in lofty fashion the supreme dignity of Jesus Christ in his person and work, in order to attack the errors of the heretical teaching that had made inroads at Colossae. Four areas where the error was manifest stand out in the letter: (1) their holding to some human philosophy, probably based on their claimed special knowledge (*gnōsis*), but definitely associated

Christ's nature and role in this most detailed explanation of such matters found in the New Testament. In him truly dwells the plenitude (fullness) of Deity (Col. 1:19; 2:9), and to him belongs the preeminence (Col. 1:18), thus denying any deity/first place to any beings of the Gnostic system.

The **Epistle to the Ephesians** is a fuller, less personal, and even formal treatment of the redemption realized in Christ and revealed in the gospel. Paul probably wrote it, like the other two letters, about the same time (A.D. 62-63), because this message also had much bearing on the doctrinal heresy plaguing Colossae. Here he described the plan which God had devised in his mind before creation, so he might bring it to fruition in Christ. In this way the "mystery" was revealed. The church, God's redeemed people,

ing of saints in Caesar's household (Phil. 1:13; 4:22), this letter went to Philippi.

Paul's Epistles During His Liberty (ca. A.D. 67)

Having already spoken about his release and later re-arrest, we shall dispense with their discussion here except to allude to such occurrences in relation to the writings of those times. Because of its important role in reclaiming Jewish converts who had begun to depart from Christ to return to Moses and because we judge it to be from the pen of Paul, we here incorporate the **Epistle to the Hebrews.** It surely originated before the fall of Jerusalem in A.D. 70, in view of its references to the continuing observance of Mosaic ordinances, persecutions against the people, and an impending catastrophe (Heb. 8:4; 10:11, 32-33; 24-25, 37). Evidence also points to its origin during Paul's liberty (Heb. 13:23). To such spiritual drifters we believe Paul sent this epistle to inform them of the surpassing superiority of Christ and his Way over Moses and the elementary foundation, upon which the gospel operated. The Law was to the gospel what the bud is to the flower. In Christ they were enjoying the fruits of the development of God's plan over many centuries, the realities only foreshadowed in the Law and the Prophets. Knowing the notoriety which Paul had gained among the Jews of Palestine and elsewhere from his prominent efforts to take the gospel to the Gentiles, we also judge the absence of the apostle's name from the epistle, both a prudent move and one of the strongest reasons for accepting it as his production. It also seems unlikely to us that a lesser personage than Paul would have sent such an anonymous letter. Many of the "church fathers," men who lived

near the time of the apostles, accepted the letter as Paul's. His references to Timothy and the others in Italy as his companions strengthen rather than weaken our conclusion (Heb. 13:23-24). The chief objection to Paul's authorship that we know is the writer's placement of himself among those to whom the word was confirmed (Heb. 2:3), but his sympathetic association with them most likely meant not personally witnessing the ministry of Jesus, not that his information had come from others. He also sympathetically identified himself with his readers in Hebrews 6:1-3 ("us"

> Hebrews "surely originated before the fall of Jerusalem in A.D. 70, in view of its references to the continuing observance of Mosaic ordinances, persecutions against the people, and an impending catastrophe."

and "we"), where he surely did not intend to say that he also still remained on the kindergarten level with his readers. Sometime in A.D. 63-64 this epistle probably went to Paul's own fleshly kinsmen through Abraham and his spiritual kinsmen in Christ. (Students might wish to consult more lengthy discussions of the authorship in other works.)

From 1 Timothy 1:3 we conclude that the apostle visited Ephesus and urged Timothy to stay there to deal with false teachings and then continued on to Macedonia, where he wrote his **First Epistle to Timothy** about such matters. He encouraged him and charged him to do the kind of teaching needed in view of the error circulating in that area. Another area of major responsibility on the young preacher's shoulders was that of developing elders (presbyters, bishops) in the

congregation. It is this interest in providing for the spiritual care of churches that has prompted most denominational writers to term these letters to preachers as "Pastoral Epistles," though elders, not preachers, are rightly referred to by the term "pastor." Crete was another stop of Paul's during this time of his life, and there he left Titus for the same purpose as leaving Timothy in Ephesus (Tit. 1:3). He may have returned to Ephesus, where he wrote his **Epistle to Titus** on his way to Miletus, Troas, and Corinth enroute to Nicopolis. Here Paul's enemies likely pressed for his re-arrest, resulting in his going back to Rome. Both of the letters written on this trip, sharing the common element of Paul's concern over false teaching and the proper organizing/equipping of local churches to cope with such problems, seem to have come forth from his pen in A.D. 67 before winter. They both also present to the two preachers their responsibilities in teaching both the lost and the saved.

Paul's Final Epistle During His Second Imprisonment (ca. A.D. 68)

From Paul's **Second Epistle to Timothy** we see evidence that the apostle's condition must have been direr than during his first confinement: (1) considered an evildoer; (2) chained; (3) deserted by friends/brethren (2 Tim. 2:9; 4:9-11, 16-17); and (4) expecting death (4:6-8). Special attention is given to strengthening Timothy for his task in perilous times, especially in relation to his timidity (1:6-14; 2:1-13; 3:14-17; 4:1-5). Most judge the letter to have been written shortly before the apostle's death in the spring of A.D. 68.

Define These Terms as Used in Relation to Paul's Life

1. Paul's daily care of the churches: _____

2. Apostle to the Gentiles: _____

3. Spirit's sanctification: _____

4. Greek religion: _____

5. Passover, Pentecost (time of year) _____

6. Righteousness: _____

7. Prison epistles: _____

8. Colossian heresy: _____

9. *Gnōsis:* _____

10. Church: _____

11. Circular letter: _____

12. "Pastoral Epistles": _____

Discussion Questions

1. How can knowledge of the situations producing Paul's letters (or other books of the Bible) help us in Bible study? _____

   _____

2. How can a book's apostolic connection show it worthy of inclusion in the New Testament?_____

   _____

3. What has this lesson demonstrated about Paul's daily care for the churches?_____ _____

   _____

4. Be able to list the four groups of Paul's letters, as classified by their time of writing, and the various letters that fit there. _____

   _____

5. Discuss the teaching of Paul about the second coming of Jesus Christ in his letters to Thessalonica. _____

   _____

6. What were some of the problems in the church at Corinth? _____

   _____

   _____

   _____

7. How are Galatians and Romans similar and different? _____

_____

8. What were some of the marks of the heretical teaching at Colossae? _____

_____

9. What bearing should Colossians 1:18-19; 2:9 have had on the speculative philosophy already at work among the Colossians? _____

_____

10. In what ways are Ephesians and Colossians similar and different? _____

_____

11. Why is there reason to believe that Philippians came forth at a time different from Paul's other prison epistles? _____

_____

12. How can lowliness (humility) prevent many of the attitude problems among brethren? _____

_____

13. What two warnings did Paul give to the Philippians? _____

_____

14. Cite the various occurrences of "joy" or a similar term in Paul's writing to the Philippians, causing us to affirm it to be a keynote of that letter. _____

_____

15. How is the Christian system the flower that developed from the Old Testament bud? _____

_____

16. Discuss the relationship between the Epistle to the Hebrews and the absence of the author's name. _____

_____

17. Why was the appointment of qualified elders so important in both Ephesus and Crete? Does that same importance continue today? _____

_____

18. How do we know that Paul's condition in Rome must have been direr when he wrote his second letter to Timothy? _____

_____

19. Do changing problems and needs in modern times justify altering the Lord's plan for organizing the local congregation? _____

20. How can the teaching of Paul in his Second Epistle to Timothy be useful in fortifying the teacher of the gospel for today's spiritual perils? _____

Bibliography

Barnes, Donnie S. *Paul, a "Hebrew of the Hebrews."* Chattanooga: Cobblestone Press, 1993.

Bruce, F.F. *International Standard Bible Encyclopedia*, "Paul, the Apostle." Grand Rapids: William B. Eerdman's Publishing Co., 1986.

Conybeare, W.J. and J.S. Howson. *The Life and Epistles of St. Paul*. New York: Anson D.F. Randolph and Company, 1877.

Free, Joseph P. *Archaelogy and Bible History*. Wheaton (IL): Scripture Press, 1962 Revision.

Goodwin, Frank J. *A Harmony of the Life of St. Paul*. Grand Rapids: Baker Book House, 1964.

Hastings, James. *Hastings' Dictionary of the Bible*. Peabody (MA): Hendrickson Publishers, Inc., 1994 Reprint.

Hayes, D.A. *Paul and His Epistles*. Grand Rapids: Baker Book House, 1969 Reprint.

Humble, Bill. *Archaeology and the Bible*. Nashville: Christian Communications, 1990.

Jenkins, Ferrell. *The Book and the Land*. Temple Terrace, Florida: No publisher given, 1976.

Keller, Werner. *The Bible as History*. New York: William Morrow and Company, 1964.

McGarvey, J.W. *A Commentary on Acts of Apostles*, Nashville: Gospel Advocate Company, nd.

Nicoll, W. Robertson. *The Expositor's Greek Testament*. Grand Rapids: William B. Eerdman's Publishing Company, 1983 Reprint.

Pfeiffer, Charles F. *Baker's Bible Atlas*. Grand Rapids: Baker Book House, 1961.

_____ . *The Biblical World*. Grand Rapids: Baker Book House, 1966.

Ramsay, William M. *The Cities of St. Paul*. Grand Rapids: Baker Book House, 1960 Reprint.

_____ . *St. Paul, the Traveller and the Roman Citizen*. Grand Rapids: Baker Book House, 1962 Reprint.

Robertson, A.T. *Epochs in the Life of Paul*. New York: Charles Scribner's Sons, 1924.

_____ . *International Standard Bible Encyclopedia*, "Paul, the Apostle." Grand Rapids: Baker Book House, 1939.

_____ . *Word Pictures in the New Testament*. Volume V, Nashville: Broadman Press, 1932.

Stringer, Johnny. *Acts*. Bowling Green: Guardian of Truth Foundation, 1999.

Tenney, Merrill C. *Zondervan's Pictorial Bible Dictionary*. Grand Rapids: Zondervan Publishing House, 1967.

Thayer, Joseph Henry. *Greek-English Lexicon of the New Testament*. Grand Rapids: Zondervan Publishing House, 1965.

Thomas, Leslie, G. *An Introduction to the Epistles of Paul*. Nashville: Gospel Advocate Company, 1955.

Vincent, M.R. *Word Studies in the New Testament*. Wilmington: Associated Publishers and Authors, 1972.

Waldron, Bob and Sandra. *The History and Geography of the Bible Story*. Bowling Green: Guardian of Truth Foundation, 1984.